My Father in Lites

A Father's Story from a Son's Perspective

The legendary Grammy award winning
songwriter, Eugene Booker Record, to the
world: singer, songwriter, arranger,
composer, engineer, producer, musician
to his family: son, brother, uncle,
husband, friend, father,

&

My Father in Lites

Written by Brian Anthony Record Sr.

Edited by Jerraine Almamie Record

&

The Record Family

D1496336

My Father in Lites

Library of Congress Control Number: 2015946798

Record Family Music Group Publishing, Chicago, IL

Cover Design by Brian A. Record Sr.
Cover Photo by Getty Images

Editions Available: Paperback, Hardback & Kindle

E-Mail: info@recordfamilymusicgroup.com

Website: www.recordfamilymusicgroup.com

My Father and I on my 11th birthday at our home

Dedication & Thanks

This book is dedicated in loving memory of Eugene Booker Record, "My Father in Lites," who performed music his entire life to support his family. Dad worked tireless hours even before his success taking a job as a cab driver.

This book is also dedicated to all my family and friends who have departed from this world.

I would first like to thank Jehovah God for not just life itself, but time, and his son Jesus Christ for a second chance of life everlasting and also the courage for such an emotional writing experience with my family. Second, I would like to thank my stepmother, Jacqueline Record, for having faith in me to help me gather important information about this book. I'd like to express my gratitude to my parents and stepparents for not only life and parenting, but for going above and beyond to continue to help steer my life in the right direction. I'd like to thank my aunt Ruthie for the love she showed us during the gathering of pictures and information. I'd like to also thank my wife, Jerraine, for to be a strong man you need a strong woman, and she has given me what I needed to become the man I am, with love, understanding, and patience.

I'd like to thank my children for enduring the pain of not having me there when they needed me. I know now as an older parent, children need their mother and father with them to steer them in the right direction and for that I am truly sorry. I also thank the mothers for having the courage and the leadership and love and endurance to raise the kids so well. Also, I thank the grandparents for understanding that the children were most important at the time and considering that to be what really mattered.

I'd like to thank my siblings for helping me to remember what was closed in my mind for some time now and the love they have shown me all my life. I'd also like to thank my cousins for continuously lifting me up and my in-laws for being there in my family's time of need, for my family would not have made it without you and for that I truly thank you and your family for their sacrifice.

My Father in Lites

CONTENTS

My Father in Lites

Introduction

Setting the Record Straight

"Oh Girl, I'd be in trouble if you left me now," or how about this, "Have you seen her, tell me have you seen her?" If you have heard these lyrics before then you have heard my father's voice, and if not, you can still read this wonderful American dream.

After my father passed away, his name soared through the media, and Dad, being so laid back, he rarely went to parties or interviews, so people didn't recognize his personal and family life. So everyone else proceeded to remain in the dark. The few interviews he did, he wouldn't divulge much on the personal side.

Later on, understanding the articles all through the newspapers and over the net, I decided to collect as much info as possible about my father because it appeared to be a variation of facts. By searching the net about my father's life, one thing stood out from all the other information about him - it was the information that wasn't there about my mother. My mother was the *Have You Seen Her* girl, the one he looked for.

You see, disappearing was the only lash of pain tool she could pass on to him, and it was enough to have him start speaking his mind about it entirely. In no way is this book written to single out anyone, but I am responsible for getting the record straight so to speak. So out of everyone who has recited the narrative every time it alters, here it is hook, line and sinker.

I searched and then I found out what subjects needed to be adjusted. It seemed as though people were guessing about my father's life and didn't recognize the truth, and low and behold it hit me - a book is needed. A bio had never been written about Dad.

His Mom and Dad were gone. My brother and I were the ones that had been with Dad and his family through his younger years, so I stepped up to the plate. Michelle, my sister, whose hobby was writing, talked about writing a bio, but she never got around to it. We lost her in death, but she did give me the idea.

The story begins at a significant time when Dad's grandfather, Mack, the musician, took his family out of Texas to move north. Booker (Mack's son) and Bernice (Eugene's parents) meet and get married and the birth of my father follows shortly thereafter. It shows how his family played such an important role in creating the right situation for his gift to evolve to what we now know to be songs of a lifetime and one of the most identifiable voices in the music industry.

This small time city boy, who almost lost his life at an early age and was a jewel of his family, found true love at an early age only to fall short of everlasting love. Not knowing or foreseeing that the pain from losing children to separating from a high school sweetheart (a ten year relationship) would flare such an anger that would set off a chain of songs that would touch millions of hearts around the world. This book is to educate people about my father's life through 64 years. It goes from him hearing music at an early age from his grandfather, Mack, and his sister, Patricia, to getting his first guitar that was given to him for Christmas that helped him write the songs. This story continues as he experiences the loss of his children, the separation from his high school sweetheart, and the train ride to stardom. Then he finds someone to soothe his heart, and he opens his eyes as he finds his Savior, Jesus Christ. It ends with his untimely death, his musical rebirth, and what's happening now.

This book has led me on a journey from sitting down with my mom's only sister, Jo Carol, to sitting down with Dad's big sister, Ruthie, and emotionally working with our family pictures knowing all the love we shared. Nevertheless, crying and getting through this writing experience has opened our family's hearts and brought us closer together knowing we had something special together that Dad gave us.

This book has opened my eyes to how important it is that the truth be stated. It has taken years to assemble the material, and it has helped me organize all that I possess. Finding out some things can put a strain on your relationship with your loved ones, things that were never talked about until now and not knowing how to put it into words without hurting anyone or scrutinizing each other as for who should take the blame if any.

The research took some time to gather from the house we grew up in to the internet, reading articles over and over and also working with my aunt and the library she has on the family as well as all that I could remember. In no way could I tell you everything about my father or every day of his life, how he spent it, but what I do tell will be the truth and most of it I shared with him and I loved him for the time he gave me.

This bio of Eugene Record is so special because I have taken the time to tell the special musical story about a true American dream. This book has taken seven years in the making, and I hope you enjoy it the most, you the one who has decided to read it.

Thank You.

MACK RECORD

Dad's grandfather, Mack, wanted more for his family by moving north, and considering the outcome, he did his family justice. He also wanted to pursue his music, but his working hours kept him from achieving that goal.

MACK RECORD

Chapter One

It's seven o'clock in the morning on the 28th of July and it's my birthday, and this is one of the most exhausting days of my life. I mean the coldest. I just turned 43 today and it should be a good day but it's not. Any other year would be great, but today I woke up and the newspapers read "Eugene Record, Chi-Lites' musical guiding force, dies." My father is gone and I won't ever see him again in this lifetime. My hero, my friend, and the only man on this earth that loved me enough to never give up on me has died.

Most of the time, you take it for granted that you will be with your loved ones all the time or maybe forever, but at some point in life, reality hits you and you find out nothing matters in this world but life itself.

As time passes by, I'm already starting to hear his songs more now than ever and it hurts. All the money in the world you could hand me would never replace my dad, my father - the one that decided that my sisters and brothers and I were worth the time and love to care about.

But if I started this story here, I would be cheating the whole world out of the truth about a lonely man who for all purpose gained stardom working hard every day and night. Not just the motorcycle, taxi driving, guitar wearing singer, but the writing, changing diapers, and just supporting us as a father does day in and day out type of dad. But a lot of that time, my mom had to "weather the storm."

For those people who want or love a good story, hold on to your britches (so to speak), relax, and get ready for one of the most intriguing stories about love, talent, and a dream that just won't end. They say music soothes the savage beast, but what if you didn't write it for that reason, but you wrote it in a release of anger, for passion and love you had for your loved one? Will it then soothe the beast in you? These writers have the talent to see inside our souls so to speak.

It's human nature to feel a certain way about a song at some point in our lives that we have heard. Say for instance, the music affects your loved ones for generations and generations to come -

not in a bad way, but more of a learning experience. The anger in your heart created an understanding and meaning that put the words together to make sense of it all.

There are many ways and reasons we write songs and compose music. Sometimes when we write songs, we like to dance and have a lot of fun. Other times, you run across a writer that expresses his life and experience in his music. Since my dad is deceased, I look at his life and personality as a judging tool to express what I feel he is trying to say. I mean, when he or she is deceased and you are a writer, you differentiate the story the best way you know how at the time of their absence. It's a therapeutic measure that encompasses an emotional release which is good for the soul. Nevertheless, Dad's songs had a date with the world, so everyone got the message and those who didn't, still can.

I am finishing this book almost ten years after my father's death because this has been a devastating experience for my family and me as well as his friends because it happened so very fast. To our family, he was just known as Dear, Dad, brother, Grandpa, and cousin, so for those who think they know what goes on backstage or at the home of a star's life, let me put those illusions to rest.

My dad came up in a hard time born during World War II to parents, Booker Record, the hard worker, and Bernice Record, the love bearer. He was the third of six kids. Patricia Record, the pianist, and Ruthie Record (Thompson), the teacher, was his elder siblings. Winona Record, Leslie Record (LP), and Janet Record were younger than Dad.

Both the love and support of his family and the experience of his life pushed his will and talent to the limits daring him to be great and in turn, forced him to the peak of the charts. Don't believe for a second that everything my father knew as a child did not bear upon his choice as well as create what would influence him into what most of the world first knew him as - lead singer, songwriter and producer of the world famous Chi-Lites. But let's not get ahead of ourselves. This story does not begin there either.

It originates in Texas on Christmas day in 1888 when Mack Record was born so you can capture the whole image. I mean, we take it for granted that we can watch television, surf the internet as well as listen to the radio and so forth. During this period in time, there was also the public lynching, torturing, and murder of Henry Smith, an African-American who was also burned at the stake in Paris, Texas.

As Mack grew, he became the child that would prove to have some musical talent that would start it all. He took guitar lessons from "the old school of hard knocks" and was very proud of his music accomplishments. Mack worked most of his life saving up for a better guitar that he had seen in the window of a department store. He was about 20 years old when the first publication of blues sheet music was printed. This was surely his era.

Mack approached adulthood in the early 1900's during the time when segregation was prominent in all facets of life in Texas for blacks. Mack and Laura "Mama Laura" Record, his wife, even lived through The Paris Fire of 1916. Whether it was in the community or on an individual basis, you were still affected by the separating of different races.

Nevertheless, they had two children, Booker and Lester. Mack, being a black strong man living in America at that time, worked hard to preserve purity and esteem among his children and his wife, Mama Laura. They would go on to raise their children with so much pride that they believed they could do and be anything they wanted.

Mack led a simple life with his wife and two boys. Sometimes he would be playing with the boys outside. Booker loved running and playing with his dad after school.

Mack worked as a porter at a young age as well as managed cotton picking and other handyman jobs. The railroads had come seven years before Mack was born, so porter jobs were available for the clean and well mannered Negroes. Every day, Mack would go down to the station for work. Everything revolved around the train station in those days, and if you missed work, you didn't eat.

Mama Laura use to knit and cook, and I would go visit her often as a kid. I loved the time I would spend with her, but that was later in her life when Mack was gone. Looking back on these times, I just sit there and think about seeing Mama Laura, knowing that the man she loved was gone and the love she would not have again. I felt helpless, but this was the start of me knowing how important family was and that we needed to look out for one another.

Now my family is known for keeping quiet about everything that goes on inside "the circle," but when business is dealing with the public, what you don't tell them they will assume or just make up the rest to fit the pieces together from the information that is out there.

The picture of Mack in this book shows him with his special tool. After years of playing the guitar, you grow accustomed to spending more for the upkeep of your tool because you have determined to abide by your craft. Uncle Leslie (Dad's brother) said that Mack had that guitar with him all the time just playing morning and night. Daddy visited him when he was a kid, but he remembered very little about Mack. He did, however, remember his guitar.

Leslie told me about the time when Mack was playing at one of the parties and it got so late Mack spent the night. It was times like this I remember spending with my family - important time, quality time.

Mack wanted to play all the time, but just like any man, he had to work a job. Back then, there weren't many different jobs for a black man to do. My grandfather (Booker) would tell me stories about Mack working in the cotton fields. Though blacks weren't slaves at the time, they still had to earn a living in some way. So whatever jobs there were, they would take them.

Cotton picking was the type of chore that made your fingers painful from touching the rugged burrs. It wasn't an easy job, but it made a living for the family. A man feels good when he's able to "bring home the bacon" regardless of what he has to do.

Mack also worked chopping wood on some occasions. See, he was not a small man, but a big and strong one, so he had quite the build for such a task.

Grandpa always told me Mack frequently talked about the day he would make money playing his guitar and that he would buy his family everything they ever wanted. However, things don't always turn out like you want them to. This aspiration of his would surely wither away.

At night, he would pray for his family and ask God to hold his family and move them in the right direction. He made his sons promise to always keep music in their family's life and Grandpa kept that promise. Music was a constituent of life for the Record family. So after enduring Texas half of Mack's life, he decided to gather his family and move north to be more prosperous. No one could imagine that one hundred years later, the Record family's dreams of being in music at that level would materialize through the seed of Mack Record.

My Father in Lites

THE RECORD FAMILY

Top row to bottom row; L-R: Booker, Patricia, Ruthie, Bernice, Eugene, Winona, and Leslie (Janet is not pictured).

THE RECORDS

Chapter Two

Booker and Bernice met at a family party, and they struck it big, fell in love, and got married. Grandpa was a hard working man. He worked at the local steel mill for years to support his family, and Bernice (Gran) worked for the United States Postal Service.

Bernice was brought up in a Christian household which makes a difference in your life. It instructs you about morals, how to conduct yourself, respect yourself, and others. The discipline of her father, Pastor Ford, helped to keep her in line which was important for the family. Her background was probably instrumental in causing Booker to be attracted to his wife when they first met. A Christian woman is always clean cut, very responsible, and of course, that love at first sight is always part of the equation when a man and a woman meet for the first time.

Like most couples, skepticism entered their minds about their future. They didn't know if they could bear children or not. No one can determine the future. All the same, they didn't appear to suffer any problems after all. They didn't waste any time creating a big family.

Booker was a tidy, hard working father who believed in waking up and going to work and being the best you can be at what you practice. In his eyes, this was the best thing for you, and it would help you stay alive. If you do your best, you probably won't get hurt on the job, and you can come home to your family in one piece.

My grandfather use to say, "You don't have sense enough to come in out of the rain." His point was that if there is trouble, you should wake up to reality that it s time to go home so you don't get "wet."

So Booker and Bernice had their first child and it was a girl - a beautiful child who was the apple of her mother's eye. This was very good for the family because when you have your first child, you feel a certain level of accomplishment.

A second child was birthed from this marriage. Her name was Ruthie. She was named after Bernice's sister. She was something very special for this household. Ruthie was so important to this household, and she had perpetually been the stronghold for the siblings. Gran always would talk about Ruthie and how she really stayed on track in school and subsequently helped her sisters and brothers if they had any problems in school. She was such a loving sister and daughter who ended up being a school teacher which suited her just fine. She has always been a great helper and a mentor whom our family always look up to until this day. As a school teacher in Chicago, she shaped the minds of young men and women into success, and she played a big role in making this book possible. She has been the mother figure to all of the grandchildren. I can invariably run to her for advice, and she steers me in the right way every time.

She always keeps her door open when it comes to family. She is so much like her mother, Bernice. She has retained all the pictures over the years. She is the most responsible one who was put in charge of keeping the family mementos. Thanks to her, they will be available for generations to come.

The third kid would be a boy named Eugene Booker Record. Gran wanted her son's name to be Eugene, and she gave him the middle name, Booker, after his father. My father, Eugene Booker Record, was a well behaved Catholic school boy. When he was a kid, he used to play with his dog and his rocking horse.

The fourth child was a girl. Her name was Winona. She grew up to become Vice President of Operations at American National Bank, and she was the reason my father and mother met. She was my mother's best friend at the time. Winona was good in school. She was one of the smart ones. I thank God for her.

The fifth child was a boy and his name was Leslie Paul Record. He was Dad's only brother, and you know brothers share secrets forever. That bond is unbreakable.

Last but surely not least, the sixth child was a young lady and her name was Janet Record. She was the baby so to speak. Janet was such a good little baby. When she was old enough to attend school, she had all her brothers and sisters to look out for her. She likewise held an advantage over her siblings because by the time she was born, her family's struggles had ceased. So she was born with a "silver spoon in her mouth" so to speak.

By Dad's big sister, Patricia, being an accomplished piano player, he frequently found himself asking her questions about music. Being one of the musicians in the home, this helped him develop and create the ear he had. You see, an ear for music is created at a youthful age, and when you nurture it, you've helped to develop your innate gift.

Dad had two wonderful big sisters, the teacher and the musician who were role models for him. His sisters used to walk with my father to the corner store (which is when he probably adopted his taste for sweets). In fact, it was the highlight of the day other than playing music together and listening to the radio.

My father's brother, Leslie, seemed to always be there when my dad needed him. He never let anyone bother him - you know, like bullies. There was one incident where some guys said something to Dad, but then they left him alone when Leslie came around because he told the guys that there would be a problem if anyone said anything to Eugene. He truly loved his brother.

LP (Leslie Paul) was a really strong person who lifted weights. Leslie would get into a lot of mishaps in his early years, but not enough that his father couldn't get him out of.

On the weekend, the kids would love to roller skate, and at this time, Eugene developed his skating skills which were extraordinary. Yes, my dad skated like he was on the ice, and this required a certain rhythm and coordination. Though Dad did not dance well, his skating skills helped him learn when he was with the group.

My daddy, just like any other child in his situation, took for granted the love he had with his kin, but as an adult, he never did to my knowledge. You know how they say "dog is man's best friend?" Well, this was truly the case with my dad and his dog. He developed a special bond with his dog, and it helped him to be more in touch with his feelings.

During Dad's childhood, his family noticed that he never expressed himself because he was sort of shy and had a laid back type of personality, so music helped him obtain room to connect his ideas in what we know today as his manifestations.

Dad would write his songs first and then compose the music around it making every accomplishment a unique, great and meaningful composition. Dad also developed his penmanship at an early age which he delivered a great writing hand and a pinnacle of a line signature that just would not stop.

You see, in our family, you don't steer too far away from the talents possessed by your ancestors. There is an old saying that blacks have rhythm, and I find this to be just so. It appeared to have evolved from years of our ancestors playing the drums in Africa. We have Indian in our descent line, and Indians are historically recognized to possess rhythm as well. With the two combinations of blood lines from Mack's family, African, and Gran's family, Indian, musicians were bound to hail from the next few generations.

As the kids started to grow up, they got into things like kids tend to do. My dad was no exception. He liked to climb trees. I never knew where I got that from until he told me. Most of the kids my dad's age didn't own a bike. However, my dad did, but he didn't really take a keen interest in riding. Since his passion was climbing things, one day he climbed over the third floor banister and fell all the way down. He was broken up pretty bad. When my grandmother got to the hospital, she was outdone. She was so hurt by this. She used to call him her number one son. My family said she barely got any sleep for days and days. Most kids would not have made it. His legs, arms and elbow were broken, and he fell on his face so his teeth came out of his mouth. However, my dad survived. Thank God for that.

Dad's elbow never healed all the way. His elbow stuck out a little bit, so it made him develop a complex about it. He would always wear long sleeves to cover it up. Dad finally recovered. This experience became a potent tool for development for him.

Now it was time for my dad to return to school. Well, as everyone knows, when a child has no front teeth, he is bound to be taunted at school, and my dad was no exception. My father didn't care about children teasing him. He said that he would have the last laugh.

He was a quiet, distinguished young man carrying a suitcase back and forth to school. This was around the same time my dad met my mother at school. My mother was in his sister, Winona's class, and she introduced Dad to Mom (Sandra Scott). However, his family did not approve of the relationship. They felt that school was more important and getting involved with girls could lead to trouble if you go too far. But Dad had good marks and was studying to be an industrial art teacher. While he was working hard day and night on his schoolwork, my mama would call him incessantly.

Dad had written songs since the age of 12. He would still write when everyone was asleep. He could actually concentrate better at that time. Dad told me he could hear a song in the traffic at night and that it formed a beat for him. He always wrote about whatever he was going through or whatever he saw.

One day, my mother told my dad that some teenagers were picking on her at school. Soon as he got wind of this, he got really angry and wanted to fight. Well, they say you should never mess with the quiet ones because you don't know what they are capable of when you "push the wrong button." He fought four guys that day, and after that, my mother said she had a newly found respect for him.

My parents were in love. They went to the coronation ball together just like in a love movie or something. My mother told me they had the time of their lives. All her classmates went to the event, and Dad picked her up in his father's car. When I look at the photo, I can just sense their passion for one another: "Just two teenage kids putting in their bids." The song, *Just Two Teenage Kids,* talks about how when my mom and dad were young and they still can remember the good times - what they did, what she was wearing, and the love. There was still a flame. This was so very special. I never knew this until I was older. It was common not to talk about my mother and father together.

At night, sometimes Dad would be playing his electric guitar without an amp and his brother would hambone on his leg and stomp making a rhythm. Dad told me after I caught him doing hambone in the studio that the rhythm has to sustain that in it for the music to have what it needs.

But just think of a young Eugene just getting his young lady friend who was seventeen, and he was only beginning to learn who he was. He now has his guitar and girl, and now he buys his first motorcycle. He's riding down the urban strip with his girl on his bike. They stop off at the soda shop, and then they go out skating with Jo Carol (Mom's sister).

Dad kept rehearsing and the women, fans, and groupies were everywhere, so Dad would drop Mom off at home, then he would go to rehearsal with "Squirrel," his best friend. He spent more time with Squirrel than anyone. This was the point when most of Dad's time was spent writing songs after school and spending time simply like any other teenager.

One time, Jo Carol asked Dad to ride, so Dad gave Mom the guitar and Jo jumped on. He started riding down the street. When he came around the corner, a bus hit the rear end of the bike, and they dropped on their left and Daddy hit his left elbow. Jo Carol got the worst of it because she fell and burned all down her arm on the asphalt. She told her grandmother she hurt herself playing because her grandma had told her not to ride on Eugene's motorcycle.

A year went by and it was time for prom, and Dad was going to take out his girl. They spent a month preparing for the event. Dad had his tuxedo and mom picked out a beautiful dress; she looked like an angel. Dad and Mom double dated with Jo and Squirrel, and they went out and ate at the Tropical Hut on the south side. Squirrel was trying to push up on Jo, but Dad didn't want that to happen. Dad was like Jo's big brother. Then they went back to the party where they had a good time.

Dad graduated from high school. A second year went by, and Dad continued to do gigs and ride his motorcycle. He also continued to sing at the competitions as well as put out a single with the Chanteurs on a local label. Gus Redmond, a close friend who lived down the street from Dad, was around at this time doing the promotion and getting the news out. Dad and Gus always talked about having their own record company.

A third year went by and Mom called Dad over to the house and met him downstairs, and they rode off on the cycle as her hair blew through the wind and her face was glowing. They stopped at the park, and Mom told Dad the news that he would soon be a father. For a moment, he just gave a proud smile, and then he wanted to celebrate. Mom had told Jo already, and when she got back, she tried to keep it secret at school as long as she could.

Dad went back home to try and explain that he was going to be a father. However, his father, Booker, was upset at him. His mom was disappointed that he was going to have a child now, but she told him she would help him any way she could. Eventually, Mom had to drop out of school because she was pregnant.

After a long talk with Marshall of The Chi-Lites (we called him "Uncle Marshall"), I learned that Dad and he were in different groups in earlier years. Dad and Robert "Squirrel" Lester were part of the group, the Chanteurs, and Marshall and Creadel "Red" Jones were part of the group, the Desideros. Marshall knew Dad was a great vocalist, but at this time, it was about winning that money on each and every show.

Now in the fifties, it was common knowledge that if you were a singing group, everyone knew who you were and your reputation. So when the battle was set for that night, everyone was there.

This one time proved to be important because Marshall's group, the Desideros, had been losing for a while now, and Dad's group, the Chanteurs, was winning time after time. Now on this day, Marshall came up with a plan to beat Dad's group. Right before the Chanteurs went on, Marshall told Red that they were going to dance a little bit before the music comes on and after Dad's group went off the stage. Marshall jumped off the stage in the air and landed on his knees, and the crowd went crazy. After they sang their song, they had gained ground. They had actually won. Clarence Johnson of the Chanteurs was mad. After a while, Dad and Clarence parted ways.

Later, one of Marshall's group members passed away, and one went into the army. The two groups broke up. Weeks later at school, it was rumored that the two groups were not together any longer. Well, one day they got together and were singing on the corner and then decided to merge as one.

They started playing at clubs. Yet, at this time, Dad had children and worked to sustain his household. But little did they recognize that one of the most successful vocal groups of all times was in the making. It's odd how things turn out for the best.

Marshall went to his uncle and told him about his plans with the group. So he told them to cut a single and he would pay for it. However, the song didn't go too far, but it gave them hope. They wanted it to be the song that would take them to the top.

My Father in Lites

Sandra and Eugene in High School

JUST TWO TEENAGE KIDS

Chapter Three

Dad got a job at the bank, but it didn't last long with him singing at night with The Chi-Lites. He couldn't get up on time, and if you knew my dad, he was a deep sleeper. You had to shake him several times to wake him. His brother told me once their family moved to another home and they were trying to wake Dad up. They moved everything in the house except Dad's bed. He finally woke up. This was a true story.

Mom and his parents were upset at Dad for choosing the group over the bank job. Dad yet continued his quest after his aspirations of having his own record label.

The sixties would prove to be very challenging for Dad. He had just recorded his first single, and The Chi-Lites' name would be born. After that first single by the group, Dad was kind of disappointed at the fact that when he put his music out to the world, he did not get a lot of feedback.

During this same time, Dad was about to become a father. While my brother was on his way, my parents decided to get married. My father started to work odd jobs around the city, and also during this time, my parents moved to an apartment on the south side.

It was 1961, and my mother was at home with Junior (Eugene Record Jr.) while Dad was working. However, my dad was looking for a better job, and he happened to run into a friend he knew who was a cab driver. So he suggested that Dad go down to the new cab station and put in for a job because about this time, Dad was working on a bigger family.

This was some of Dad's good times with Mom. They had one child and Dad was working. Mom wanted to go back to school, but Mom got pregnant with me (Brian). So she started to get ready to have another baby.

After Mom had me, it was the summer of 1962. Michelle was the next to come less than one year later. That means Mom barely got over the previous pregnancy before she was pregnant again. The family was growing fast to say the least.

Michelle was the first girl, so this was a special time for my father. His first baby girl who when she became older felt she never experienced the love she deserved from her mother and father.

Next, Vincent was born; I have always wondered about him and was there any song about him. I have always had my brother, Eugene Jr., who for some time was with me always. You see, we were together no matter where we lived and so were Michelle and Angela. I know we would have had so much fun together. I could imagine him looking something like both of us. To picture my brothers and one not being there is horrifying to say the least. My parents, who are righteous, look at all the children the same.

Why him and not me I ask from time to time. Perhaps we could have been like The O'Jays. I say them because they are one of my favorite groups. Eugene Jr., Vincent and I performing in a group, "E.B.V.," who knows, but just maybe that could be the special thing that has yet to come from the most high.

Mom and Dad lost their son in such a short time, and knowing my parents like I do, they sat there and just prayed with their friends just looking at him and asking God to have mercy on his soul. I can even feel the pain as I type and cry and imagine smiling at his face just to let him know we love him and that everything is going to be alright because the old things will pass away. That's the comfort that everyone wants as a child.

As days go by, the first week, you are just coming to grips of the whole thing that he may not make it, and no matter what the doctors say, the mother and father still feel with God, there is always hope.

As they go through the second week, Dad is still working and meeting Mom at the hospital, and the three kids are at grandmother's house. Dad was 23 and Mom was 22, and she had just had her birthday while at the hospital. It was very emotional for her all that was happening at the same time.

By the third week, things started turning for the worse. There were signs that Vincent was going to be on his way to heaven. Dad and Mom continued to pray for him. Of course, my siblings and I didn't remember him until I started writing this book. Through the family and my eyes, bringing the truth to the surface can be painful at times, but you acquire exactly what you are looking for when you look for the truth.

Vincent was born on July 10th and died four weeks later. It was really painful for the young couple to witness the look on our little faces. The children don't really know the impact of what's going on, so you suppose maybe it won't be so difficult for them, but little do they know, all things "crack the surface" eventually.

Angela, my sister, was born next and she was a darling child. She was very small like Mom and as cute as can be. This made five children in six years and the loss of one. This created quite a challenge for the family. Dad was having more shows at this time, and Mom was taking care of the children. Mom even got a babysitter so she could go to a show. Mom showed up one day and made a scene with one of the fans who were grabbing on Dad on stage. She was very jealous of all the groupies.

The next child was Darlene. She was born with Hyaline Membrane Disease which is called RDS now and that stands for Respiratory Distress Syndrome. This frequently is found in premature infants caused by developmental insufficiency of surfactant production and structural immaturity in the lungs. This was their sixth child. I know getting this information from the doctors was devastating to my parents after losing their son, my brother, Vincent, three years earlier. This had to be the hardest news ever in their lives because with Vincent, he lived only four weeks, but this event was soon to take them on a down ride that would not be favorable at the end. I can only imagine the long hours that my parents stayed at the hospital and the pain of not knowing if this would be her last time being there or if she was coming home.

The disease makes breathing difficult, and sometimes this panics the parents into rushing the child to the hospital. I'm pretty sure Dad took Darlene in the cab at some stage, and the ambulance came several times through the night. Being the wonderful parents that they were, they stayed tireless hours with her without the other children knowing what was even taking place. At this time, my brother, Junior, was only seven years old. I was five years old. Michelle was four years old and Angela was two.

This I'm sure, put a great strain on the family, fighting for the life of their baby, and at the same time, taking care of the other children who were soon to be in school. Junior was already going to school, and our grandparents had stepped in to support the family at this point by taking him to school on a regular basis.

Night after night, my mother for two whole years fought for the health of my sister. She fought through the treatments and checkups just trying to hear some good news about the tests they continued to run on Darlene. Time after time, the news went up and down. Sometimes she was doing good and other times it was disappointing.

The children, being so young, except my brother Eugene, never knew what was going to hit them at the time and never knowing that what was about to happen would change their lives forever.

Most people take it for granted that when someone dies in the family, you all mourn, then you move on. However, this is not so. Not only was my father going to try and write his pain away, but he wanted the whole world to know how much pain he was in.

Darlene was born in 1967, and as the time passed on, Dad would meet Barbara Acklin. With the relationship starting to strain with Mom, he found himself in *Someone Else's Arms*.

Life has always had a double standard for men and women. When a man cheats, he is a player, but when a woman cheats, she is called out of her name. I am not taking sides in no way because when a person commits adultery, it is one in the same in God's eyes, so I see it the same way. Since we have to live by the sword so to speak, it's him you have to answer to.

The song, *Someone Else's Arms,* Barbara and Dad wrote, could not have come at a better time exposing the relationship. The song comes in and states, "You want to say goodbye, I want to say goodbye, but my heart just won't let me" - of course, this is a relationship that is on the brink of destruction. "One day I'm going to fool you and I'm going to go to someone else's arms" - I can see that the relationship was falling apart right before their very eyes. Dad found comfort in the arms of his fellow writer.

All the same, like we all experience when you find consolation in this world, it is just for a short time. Afterwards, reality hits and then you come back down entirely to see that your kid is still here sick, and it's back to the hospital again and again, and the relationship has yet to be dealt with. The start of Dad writing with Barbara and signing with the company, Brunswick, may have cast his career on a cloud. However, that cloud was going to pass down some because Darlene was getting sicker by the months, and at this time, there was nothing in the universe that would stop this train from wrecking.

At this time, Darlene became a full-time job for Mom, so my sisters, Michelle and Angela, started staying with Dad at Barbara's house. Mom decided to go on with her life, and Darlene was her main concern.

In the song, Dad shows that he is not ready to take on another relationship because his heart doesn't know where to start. He had been in a relationship since high school, and if anyone has been in that position, they know it's hard to start another relationship at the snap of a finger. You are so used to that person. The love is so strong because you actually have grown up together from childhood, and you are in a lot of ways alike in most of what you do. Dad didn't go looking for love. It kind of came to him so to speak.

At the big change, Dad says, "Here's to the pain you brought me, here's to the ring I brought you, here's to the time I wasted, and here's to the tears I've tasted." Dad was very hurt and definitely accusing Mom of infidelity and not wanting to be with him anymore. However, Dad doesn't want to go to anyone else, but was being forced to. If he wanted love, he would have to find it somewhere else. Barbara had just got out of a relationship as well. This could have been what they had in common. This may be true since they both sang this song, *Someone Else's Arms*, on each one of their albums.

The winter was very cold during 1967. They called it The Blizzard of 1967 and Darlene was with Mom. Of course, Dad was back and forth from her home. Darlene was now a year old, and we were going into the next winter in 1968, but this would prove to be the heaviest hit. Darlene had turned two years of age on January 27, 1969, which at this time, her health took a turn for the worst. Her health started to decline, and the doctors talked to my mom and dad to let them know she would have to be hospitalized for some time to see if anything could be done. The couple waited anxiously for Darlene's recovery for weeks only to fall short. Darlene died in April, the spring of 1969.

The next day, my brother and I got a call from our mother to tell us our sister Darlene had died. My brother and I were young at the time and did not understand what she was telling us, or let's just say I didn't.

My father came and picked us up, and we went to the funeral. My mother was upset at him for bringing us, but we were happy to be with him. I recall walking into a situation which I later understood was the funeral home, and my mother was crying and screaming. We walked toward her, and you could tell by her facial expression that she was really furious.

I saw my little sister in that box, and it changed me forever. When I went to school the next week, I talked to my teacher and friends about my sister. My grandmother got a call from the school to ask about me getting some type of counseling.

I've never seen my father in so much pain before. Even though I was young, I could see his anguish.

Constantly thinking about what my sister looked like, Darlene, trying to put her image in my mind and straining to recall how she looked is so tough. Sometimes it is overwhelming. My parents' pictures were destroyed a long time ago, and no one kept any pictures of her that

I have found. So when I look at my brother and sisters, I can barely imagine her. I think my dad saw her in us as well.

My father never talked about his daughter, so he put it down in words. Every day for years, I listen to *The Coldest Days of My Life*. It wasn't until I was writing this book that I started really listening to the song's words. It wasn't cold in the spring. "The signs of springtime" is, of course, in the spring, so with all the research data right in front of me, I learned that Darlene, my sister, passed away in the spring. Listening to *The Coldest Days of My Life,* this song seems to have some of Dad's words about Darlene: "With eyes of a child shining so bright and take away the pain."

I mean, my father started talking to God in this song. You had to have missed someone very special in death to make you so angry that you scream at God about down under. "Voices suddenly reminded me that she's gone," and instantly I pondered over the fact that my father had just gotten his first hit song, but Darlene's death was surely a blow to our family. We would all never be the same. Parents sometimes can't pick up the pieces in the relationship. Sometimes there is blame, and other times, the pain is just too much to bear.

Dad, through all of this, was coming down in the basement of my grandmother's house writing. My brother and I used to sit on the stairs listening to him play. Time after time, we would hear him sing, and sometimes he would let us join in and play. These were the times I will never forget.

Dad wrote a song called *To Change my Love* on his first album on Brunswick. Here he clearly sees evil in the world as he explains that the world is full of broken hearts. People are jealous and envious, and hate is seeping into the relationship. People are alleging the woman does not love him, and this is one of those short two minute songs. It goes right to the spot, but after listening to what is said, it is clear that the relationship is accepting its first blows.

You're no Longer Part of my Heart was so important in my father's life because at the time, he was pulling away from the relationship, so I get it. The relationship doesn't stop there. It proceeds along another plane of respect. There has to be stability between the mother and father for the sake of the children.

It was the tip of the iceberg when it came to my parents love for each other since there was pain felt from the words that were written in this song. People going through the same situation can relate to the lyrics. As it said in the song, it was a reality - "like my ship is going out to sea never to return." The fire she put in his heart burns. This is love, a broken heart.

It gets pretty ugly, and the song shows just the opposite feelings was going on - he did care. The song begins when the companion has shown a sign of infidelity. The one who struck first knows at this time it is on. "So many nights I spent alone because you lost your way back home" - Dad's words in this song actually hit home. I mean, Mom was sometimes a no show from the stories on how we ended up in Gran's home.

This song, *I Reached Out to You,* represents the grim side of what love can do if you love someone more than yourself.

In the song, *Your Love Drifted All Away,* the tension that was going on is even painful for me to hear without getting emotional. This is the life I have to hold on to. See, I was so young back then that I couldn't enjoy my parents together, but when I listen to the music, it brings them back together. Yes, my parents had a lot of hard times, and since I didn't have much time with them together, I bring them together in this book to share with the world. "The part I played as a man has been turned into a grain of sand" - come on, this guy has had enough of whatever he is receiving on the other end.

I know some people may think, does this guy think all these songs are about his mom? I say yes, if I point it out, but Dad's first album is written between 1965 and 1968. During this time, trouble started with Mom and Dad one year after the death of their son, my brother, Vincent. Every song is about this woman that has got him uptight.

Now this next one was my grandmother's favorite song of my father's on this album, *What Do I Wish For*. This song sure shows not only the love he had for her, but the enslavement she has him in. He states in the song, "I wished I never met you," and at the same time telling her, "I love you too much." This is way out slave love. You can't get out of it no matter what. His words, "I can't stand the things about you but still in love," is like being under shackles and pad locks. Even the songs Dad didn't write, he is still trying to get back with this woman. I believe when Dad and the record company found out people started listening to this broken heart, he kept right on writing because it wasn't hard at all.

The words in this song, *24 Hours of Sadness*, lets you know the woman still didn't come home. She has been a bad girl. He said she was missing, and he doesn't know where he can find her. She is really taking him for a ride. He said he wished he could find her, so still he misses her even more and still wants her back no matter what. On that first album when Dad sang someone else's songs, the story never varied. *My Whole World Ended* and *The Twelfth of Never* are two songs from the album Dad didn't write, but the account is nevertheless there. There is one song in particular that every time I listen to it, I fall apart because no matter what day it was, Dad would step up and prove to be a more honest individual. The song is *Yes I'm Ready if I Don't Get to Go*. How could you be mad at someone that despite their shortcomings that we all have, they wake up and love as hard as they can?

In this song, Dad had been under attack just by people around him. He sang this song as if he was being held down, nice and subtle, never loud, as the background continued to act like horns echoing into a fade.

When my father wrote *Yes I'm Ready if I Don't Get to Go*, it was hard to believe that within eight years, his marriage had failed, two children had passed, and his music career was standing still which is enough to make someone with unimaginable songwriting talent write down the emotions he was going through.

Give it Away was The Chi-Lites' first top 40 hit. Not surprisingly so, for Dad's marriage at this time was on rocky grounds. In the song, he states, "What's the sense in giving you love when you're going to give it away?" He also felt that no matter what they went through, she would still be his.

However, at this time, he was having a relationship with Barbara Acklin, his writing partner. Shortly after that, he met soon to be wife, Jackie Sutton. The song also states, "You say you have nothing to live for." During that time, after my mother lost her two children, she stated to my dad that she didn't want to live and had started to drink a little too much. When my mother saw that Dad had people in his life that were moving him forward, she didn't want to get in the way, so she vanished. She also had gotten with a crowd that kept her running the streets, and by now, my father had received a call from her to come and get the children because she had enough.

The song, *Are You My Woman (Tell Me So),* states in the beginning, there is a problem about who you belong to, stating that Mom had another at this time as they were having an up and down and in and out relationship. He also states that he may have to go to jail because he is going to hurt whoever it is. Dad also said that "she set his soul on fire"; there's that fire in his heart and soul again. This message was the last straw, and this lets you know that both are confused about where the relationship is now, but soon time would tell.

One day, my mom left us at home (which would later prove to be for the last time), and told my dad, who was on the road, that she couldn't take it anymore. The police came along with my grandfather and my uncle Les Paul to our apartment. It took them an hour to get my brother, Eugene Jr., to open the door and let them in. My brother has always been overprotective of his family. My brother and I went to stay with my grandpa and my grandma. Michelle and Angie went back to stay at Barbara Acklin's house again, and Dad went back and forth. Dad was working for Brunswick at the time and doing shows in and out of town, so Barbara watched over the girls and we were separated again.

At the time, I didn't understand why or what was going on, but it would change my life forever.

Eugene with his parents, Bernice and Booker

MY GRANDPARENTS

Chapter Four

The first year I started living with my grandparents, I was too young to attend school. My brother was in first grade, and my family, for the first time, was not with me. My father was working and singing.

My mother was not in my life. My sisters were living at Barbara Acklin's house, and my brother went to school every day. I would wait at the window every day for him. As I grew up, I realized why I did that. What else would a kid do after his family was taken from him overnight?

It was the year 1967, and I was finally old enough to go to school.

This was the same time my parents went through their relationship. School was new to me. I didn't understand a lot. There was no preschool at the time. My parents weren't available to aid me with my homework. My brother tried to help me to no avail. At this time, my father was recording his LP, and he was about to make history in a couple of years.

During that school year in 1968, Dr. Martin Luther King Jr. was assassinated. When I went to school, they talked about his death in class. We got out of school early that day because there was a lot of violence in the streets.

On my way home, I was hit with a brick in the forehead. When I came home to my grandma, she was crying, and she took me to the hospital to get all patched up. She also called my father and he came to see me. I came back and we followed the news all weekend about Dr. King. I was five years old when he was killed. I was in kindergarten then. My grandma rocked me to sleep that night. She would always do that when I was not feeling well.

My grandmother rocked me to sleep until I was eight years old, and she called me her "Briany doll." My father said she spoiled me and made me soft; I say she taught me what love really was. See when she got me, she had already raised six children and did a wonderful job at that.

Well, when she got me, I was a little messed up. I would cry myself to sleep almost every night. I didn't realize why at the time. Maybe I did and was too young to handle it. It was probably because of my mother.

Grandpa would take me to the park at the university by 61st Street. It was so big! I just ran all day with my brother. You know he was my best friend of all time. I never recall him being without me or me being without him. My grandfather would always bring us to the park together, not one without the other. We would go to the store on the corner of 73rd and Luella.

We would get some potato chips, soda and some bubble gum from the corner store; I remember it just like it was yesterday. I guess some things you never forget, especially when you have such a wonderful time. I also remember my uncle LP who was always there for me. He never let me down. He would pick me up real high in the air, and then put me down. Up and down I would go.

While I was in the house, I would play on the back porch most of the time. I would have so much fun. In the evening, I would watch TV with my grandparents in their bedroom. We would look at Tom Jones. Some of my grandma's favorite songs by him were *What's New Pussy Cat* and *It's Not Unusual*. Those were the songs she would sing. My grandpa would drink his Budweiser and smoke his Pall Mall cigarettes.

We first saw the Jackson 5 on The Ed Sullivan Show. We saw these kids on television singing and dancing, and we would always say we wanted to do that as well. Never did I think that I would actually be doing that when I got older and would have been in the same room with these guys.

One of the most controversial times in my father's life is when he and my mother got married (she was very young) and the timeline on meeting Barbara and Jackie. We were youngsters, but we knew something wasn't right a few times, and those times were confusing to watch as a kid. Of course, no marriage is perfect. However, if it's hard on the children, parents have a duty to either talk to them or get them counseling.

Dad and Mom must have separated during her pregnancy with Darlene or during her illness. At this time, Dad had began writing with Barbara, and then he met Jackie as she worked at Chess Records down the street from his office. People just assumed Dad and Barbara were married because you never saw my mother. Mom had lost what she loved and couldn't be hurt anymore.

I remember playing in front of my grandmother's house when Darryl Gordwin said, "Brian, your dad is on TV. Come and see!" I ran so fast up his steps, and when I got in the living room, I was so shocked to look and see my father in that black box singing *Let Me Be the Man My Daddy Was*. I couldn't believe it! This was more than simply a dream come true because I can remember drawing Dad in my classroom just days earlier, and my teacher, Ms. Red, took it from me.

When I was at my grandma's home, my aunt, Candy (Janet), was living there along with her son, Donald Broome, and her daughter, Kimberly Broome. Aunt Janet would be in her room with her two kids. They were my friends as well as my cousins. My uncle, LP, was down the street from our home, and his son, Randolph Record, was with him as well. We had so much fun at Christmas time hanging out with each other. I remember the night before Christmas, Donald and I would stay up all night and wait for my grandfather and LP to get the toys out of the basement and bring them upstairs. During that time, I really thought Santa Claus was real. So when my cousin, Donald, told me that he was not real, I really flipped.

I didn't know why they would have told me something that was not true. I was so naïve thinking that there really was a Santa Claus. I feel if it is not the truth, kids should not be told that. They need to know the truth about life from the very start like about credit reports, social security, and why you need to go to school to get a good job.

With my father, composing was like a new invention to him and recording was about getting that song he wrote on tape the best way he knew how. You see, Dad was a true songwriter and music composer. He took his guitar, sat down, and with his pen, he directed the whole song from that legal sized sheet of paper. Anyone who has written a song before knows that a regular sheet of paper is not long enough to hold the entire song on the front sheet, but the legal size is just right. You can put your name of the song and your verse, bridge, chorus, and so forth on it.

Now, once he got his words down on paper, he began arranging his guitar. You see, he would already be hearing the song and playing along with it as he penned it down. He was starting to finalize the guitar on tape, and he would scat along with it as he put it down on tape.

Today, I still have the tapes, and when I play them, I imagine him sitting there in his chair like it was just yesterday. You see, this was the time that my siblings and I could sit on the stairs and listen. I stated earlier, we would be there to hear the songs being created. I mean, this was our time with him when he would be creating music for the world to embrace and enjoy and for us. It was such an amazing feeling hearing a song being created and then over time seeing it transform into a masterpiece with strings, horns, and the works.

When my mom was younger, she told us Dad would write her letters to make up with her. When they grew older, he still sent letters, but she stated that she didn't reply to them.

On this particular occasion, I was in my bedroom sleep, and I heard the bell ring over and over again. Then I heard a loud noise coming up the stairs. It was my aunt Pat. My grandfather said that she had been drinking and she needed to go home, but she started to fight with him. After my grandma called the police and they came to take her away, we all had to get up and get in Grandpa's car and go to the hospital.

At first, I thought she was hurt. Nevertheless, later in life, I was told that she suffered a nervous breakdown, and she had been a mental patient for quite some time.

Usually, I would see Pat come on Sunday morning and play the piano. Yes, every Sunday morning I would wake up to her playing the piano. She was so good. She played like no one else I knew. She would play gospel music that somehow took me to another place and time. Every week I would come in there and sit down. She had a special name for me. She called me "Dew" just like the morning. I never knew why she called me that, but one day I hope to find out.

Pat never combed her hair, and it seemed exactly like Don King's hair. People would laugh at her when she would leave and walk down the street, but not me. I loved her so much for what she gave me and what she taught me and who she was to me. This is called respect.

You see, she and I had something in common; she was displaced for something she had gone through, and so was I. I felt like I was different. Every one of my cousins was with their parents at this time, either their mother or father, but I wasn't. I felt that I had done something wrong and that I had to be punished for it.

Every Sunday I saw her come and play, I started feeling her pain in the notes she was playing, the beat she kept the whole time, the 10 to 20 cigarettes she would smoke in just two hours, and the perspiration that would fall from her head which would relieve her somehow to get through to the next week. We never really talked, but I could see that we had started a relationship without saying a single word. She would just look at me and say, "Dew. Hey, Dew." I cried every week she left and I didn't know why.

I would go outside and play every day while we were at my grandma's house. My great grandma, Gertrude Ford, lived downstairs when

I got there. She would say I looked just like my mother. When I would go downstairs, she would only render me a look. After she passed, my cousin, Nona, came to live downstairs with us.

I remember it like it was yesterday how the events unfolded this particular day, from a lovely morning with my grandparents to an incident that could have caused Dad to suffer the loss of another child, me.

My brother and I woke up to a morning breakfast with our grandparents. Gran always made breakfast for us, but it was special on the weekend. The smell of bacon, eggs, toast and hot coffee percolating on the stove was in the air calling us to the table. My clothes were always clean, pressed and folded in the drawers. Gran made sure we brushed our teeth and gargled with Listerine. Then off to the kitchen we would go. Gran always told us to pray and be thankful for our food. This was a "golden rule" in her house.

My cousins, Donald and Kimberly, were there with us as well. After breakfast, we would watch television. There were no video games at the time, so we mostly played with our toys or went outside to ride our bikes.

Gran got a call from Uncle Leslie, and he said he was going to the park for a picnic and wanted to know if my brother and I would like to come. We said, of course, we'd love to come with him. Gran went to our room to get our things out and then we got ready.

Leslie had come back from Germany. My uncle was serving honorably during the Vietnam War, and while stationed in Germany, he met and fell in love with Sonya Knoedler.

They got married, had a baby named Randolph, and moved here.

Once we were ready, we went in the living room to wait for Uncle Leslie to arrive. He bumped the horn, so we went outside to meet him and got in his car which we loved - a new '69 blue Dodge. We were going to the beach and park at 53rd Street Hyde Park Beach by The Museum of Science and Industry. I loved that place at one time, but that was about to change for me.

My uncle was cooking while my brother and I were playing. It was a beautiful summer day outside, perfect beach weather with no rain in sight. While Uncle Leslie was cooking, he was tending to his family. This was nothing out of the ordinary because we weren't young children. I was about seven or eight years old and my brother was around nine or ten years old.

I was at the beach with my uncle, LP and his wife, Sonya, and their son, Randy, and my brother. Sonya was from Germany, and before she came, she would talk to me on the phone and tell me she would see me when she got here. When she made me a green knitted sweater and a German chocolate cake, I was in love.

My brother and I were playing on the rocks at the beach. I slipped and fell in and went under. My brother went to tell my uncle. They came back and I was still under water. I could see my brother, but I could not get up because of the seaweed. My uncle held my brother's legs and stuck him in the water. He grabbed my hands as I reached up. My brother saved me. Yes, he saved my very own life. He has always been overprotective. I could not be out of his sight after that. No one until this day knew about this but us.

When my dad bought his new purple drop top Cadillac, I was still at my grandma's house. He would come by and let me know that it would not be long before we would be a family again. He was going to buy us a house, and we would be together once again. I was so happy when he told me this. I was about eight or nine years of age during this time. That year on my birthday, he bought me a purple bike to match his car. I was so excited. This was the best present I had ever received. I would ride that bike every day, morning until night. I had a small front wheel and a large wheel in the back. I loved that bike.

One day, my friend Teddy and I were riding down the street and some boys tried to take my bike from me. I started to ride as fast as I could.

Faster and faster I went. They could not catch me. When I got back home, I put my bike in the vestibule like always and Teddy and I went upstairs to get some Kool-Aid. When we came back downstairs, my bike was gone. I was so crushed. I cried for about a week. We walked around the neighborhood for two weeks looking for it, but we never saw my bike again.

During this same time, my brother and I had our first dog and his name was Toby. My dad wrote a song named after our dog. When we first got him, he was just a puppy. He was white and beige. We played with him every day. One day when we were playing with Toby, he ran out into the street and got hit by a car. He did not die right away, but a short while later the veterinarian came and had to put him to sleep. This is something else that I loved that left this earth too early.

When I was with my grandma, she would always say that I was a dancer. When my grandma's friends would come over, my grandma would have me dance for them. She would always make me feel like I could do anything. She was truly a jewel. She was a very special person, and not just to me, but to everyone that knew her.

I remember when we would go to Three Rivers, Michigan every summer to visit Gran's sister's house, Ruth, and her husband, Miller. Her house was in a beautiful area. As soon as we would get out the car, we would run down the hill. It was about two blocks to the bottom of the hill, but felt like three, and you could fish and have a boat in the lake. Miller would have our fishing rods. It was so hot and the food and family was the best. Gran would bring her famous apple sauce. The day just seemed like it would last forever.

One of the special times that I shared with my grandmother was when we would go to church. I remember her asking me if I wanted to go with her. We would walk to St. Phillips Neri Catholic Church on 72nd Street just a couple of blocks from the house. I loved sharing that time with my grandma. I don't remember much about what the priest was saying. I just remember I was with her, so I knew everything was fine. She had a good heart, so I knew she would be in God's memory when she left here some years ago.

On the way home, we would talk about how my father was working for my brother and me and that he would soon come and get us and we would be a family. I was told I should get on my knees and pray for this to come to pass. I did just that as far back as I can remember.

Sundays was also very special to me because we would eat a very big meal, and boy could my grandma cook. Every now and then, we would see someone extra at the table on this day, my aunt Pat. I was starting to discover that family was everything. The love I had for everyone and the love they had for me was felt everyday in my life. I just didn't know all that was about to take a major turn when I was to move into the house my dad would buy.

Mom came to see us one day when Dad was out of town, and my grandfather had told her not to come, so she had it out with Grandpa. This was truly a roller coaster ride, and the children had no other choice but to ride.

When you think about it, everyone has their day because no one is perfect. Every time I hear a story about someone, I want to know their good points and their bad points so I can weigh it all out and determine if he or she is a righteous person, and even then, you will never get the right story all the way. Something will always be left out and sometimes on purpose. The family was on their way, a new era.

My Father in Lites

Eugene Record

BRUNSWICK

Chapter Five

I remember my father getting home with his checkered taxi cab cap on and calling out to us. We would all just run up to him and he would hold us. We didn't want to let go of him. There was so much love in the room. He would fall asleep right there with us in his arms.

See, my father was working and trying to do his music at the same time. His aspiration for us was constantly there. It was his motivation to keep going. I could see this coming from a man that was taught by his father that taking care of his children was number one.

After signing with Brunswick in 1968, they released the number ten R&B hit, *Give It Away.* This horn and funk mid-tone song was one of the family favorites.

Carl Davis knew talent when he saw it. The Chi-Lites were put right in his lap, and Eugene Record was "heaven sent" for a producer like Carl. We know Carl made some calls that night, and when the morning came, Dad was writing and producing. While Carl produced, Dad wrote and vice versa.

Carl also knew that the group needed some grooming. You see, groups need exposure to doing live shows and studio, so it took them about a year before they were ready. Meanwhile, Dad started producing with Carl. They released some of the hottest tracks that are still selling and being remade today like *Soulful Strut* and *Love Makes A Woman.* Dad co-wrote and

produced these songs while recording
The Chi-Lites. He wrote for nine or
ten recording artists before putting
out The Chi-Lites' first album. Dad
began writing for Jackie Wilson,
Barbara Acklin, The Lost Generation,
Peaches & Herb, Young-Holt Unlimited,
and the list goes on. He was writing
so much that the second Chi-Lites'
album only had a few new songs. Dad
was an established hitmaker before
his first Chi-Lites' album.

His first break was producing
and writing for Brunswick which
established him forever as a
producer, writer, musician, arranger,
and singer, a record company's dream.
It would earn him a Vice President
office right next to Carl's. They
even wrote for other record labels
because they had an interest in their
talent as well.

When Dad finally slowed down and
concentrated on The Chi-Lites, he

produced and wrote the most successful two albums of The Chi-Lites, their third and fourth album – *(For God's Sake) Give More Power to the People* and *A Lonely Man*. Dad and Carl had a very special business relationship and spent years working together. Later, after the success of those two albums, Dad made the front cover of Blues and Soul magazine that held him "Eugenius."

Dad met Jackie Sutton, who worked down the street from his office at Chess Records. He fell in love with her and made her his wife. Jackie was a hard act to follow, had the right upbringing, studied very hard and if I can remember, continued to go to school during her time at home. Everybody was in school, but Dad. Jackie helped Dad balance his family even though it required some time. Dad was used to recording all the time or doing live shows. Even though it paid the bills, the house had to be attended to. So they hired a maid. Her name was Janie.

Dad was such a clean person, and Jackie did well by us. She was good with kids, just a little nervous at first, but we adored her. I would see Jackie interacting with my sisters as they played with their dolls and wigs. She spent quality time with us as a family.

What was really exceptional about my dad is that he knew when to give his children some of his time. He would come home from recording all day, maybe all night, but he made sure he would look in on his children. I remember barely being up and Dad would look in on us; even though he was gone a lot, he let us know the love he had for us. He had a picture of his children in his wallet. He loved us all! The song,

Let Me Be The Man My Daddy Was, is a reflection of his love for us.

Have You Seen Her was about my mother, Sandra. She left and never came back. But *Oh Girl* was about my stepmom who he met and fell in love with. Funny how the songs that means so much to a person turns out to be the strongest and biggest sellers. The truth is always the most heartfelt.

Many times we would be at the studio downtown Chicago, and the musicians would take a break. I would go on the drums and play. I enjoyed the drums because early in my life, Dad used to record with my brother and I.

Dad also produced a song called *The Sly, Slick and The Wicked* that tied for trade publication record World's 1970 Record of the Year award with The Jackson 5's *ABC,* which was a great accomplishment for a newcomer.

As children, we got to share some experiences with some of the best musical geniuses in the world who came through the studio at Brunswick and Universal, as well as the home studio.

Dad came home one day and said that we would be the Jackson family's guest at their show Saturday and it was Wednesday. I could not wait to see Michael and his brothers. As a kid, I saw them for the first time on television.

Now when I went to school, I found out my sister had told everyone. So I had messages for Michael from all of my friends. One guy even asked me if he could go in my place.

That Saturday, we met the Jackson family. I played pinball with Randy. My brother socialized with Michael, and my sisters were in astonishment the whole time. Having my father at home was a dream come true and meeting and hanging out with some of the stars topped it all from a kid's perspective.

Now Dad's album came out. It was a big thing. My stepmom (Jackie) said a new contract meant a new house. My grandmother took me and my brother into the room and said that our dad was coming to get us. Do you know how that felt for me? I had been waiting for seven years to hear just that. Even though my father had come to see us as often as he could, this would prove to be different. You see, we were dressed up in our suits and very tearful.

The doorbell rang and for some strange reason, it was different this time out of all the times it had rung before. My father appeared from the stairs and told us to come on. We all smiled and he told my grandma, "Thank you for all that you have done for me, Momma."

My father hugged his mother so tight, and you know, as I pulled away from my first home and the love of my life, my grandmother (but just "Gran" to me), never to spend the time with her that I wanted, I realized I had grown so attached to her that it was an emotional experience for me.

My father began to appear on television shows like The Flip Wilson Show, American Band Stand and Soul Train. Dad was either writing in the studio, recording TV shows, or on tour performing.

We moved into our new house just three and a half blocks from my grandma's house. My dad was working on the basement while we skated down there with the skates my mother bought us. We were sleeping on the floor until we got our beds. However, we didn't have to wait very long. My brother and I had our own room.

This was in 1972. During this time, my father had one of the biggest LP's out. Nevertheless, in our mind, he was just Dad and we were with him. That's all we wanted.

Moving into the house with Jackie was new to us. My sisters called Jackie "Momma," but my brother and I called her Jackie. We did not like the idea of my dad with this woman, but we learned to love her. Most kids want their mother and father to stay together for the rest of their lives, but that does not happen all the time. I did not hold that against her, but I felt that she was kind of young to have four kids that she was suddenly responsible for. Nevertheless, she had to have loved my father to take care of all of us. That would have been really challenging for anyone.

The first year there, we started school at Our Lady of Peace. We made new friends and everything. Michelle and I started guitar lessons with the nuns. Angie took piano lessons. The girls were also enrolled in dance school because Jackie's dad was Tommy Sutton, and he owned his own dance school. The girls would go to dance on Saturday. On Sundays, we would go to the show and see movies like Super Fly and Bruce Lee movies or go skating.

Every Christmas was very special. The first Christmas in our new house, our father bought us a pinball machine. Our father made sure that we had everything we needed. He was very overprotective of his kids. The world had him, but he did not want to give us to the world. Everything was perfect. Still, there was something that troubled me.

When we would go and visit my mother, she lived in this small basement apartment. When my father told me we were going to be a family again, I thought it was going to be with my mother, father, sisters and brother. At first, we had to learn to get along with our new mother. This was a big adjustment for her as well as us. My dad knew that if Jackie was going to take on this responsibility, she would have a lot on her. So if we got into a disagreement with her, he would have to give her the benefit of the doubt. After all, she was taking on a big job.

I had a problem with now being a kid and having events that my mother, father, stepmother, or stepfather would not attend. At an early age, a child needs encouragement; it's important that he or she receives it, but we never did. It seemed like everyone was living their life, and the children just got whatever was given to them.

As a kid, I was a lot like my dad when he was little. I never talked back to my parents. Even until this day, I have never raised my

voice to any of my parents in their
house or outside of it. Sometimes, I
think I should have because I held it
in all this time, but I believe
writing this book is the most
effective way to express myself.

Getting back to my mother in her
small basement apartment, we had so
much fun with my mother at her place
on 63rd and Green Street in Chicago.
Although it was not the big house,
the love she showed me was something
that I missed all those years. I
never knew what I was missing when I
was at Gran's house.

My mother would always hold us
tight every time we would go there.
She won the lottery one time. She
didn't win much money, but it was
enough to take us shopping. It had
snowed a lot and it was cold, so she
turned on the stove to heat the
basement up. I remember we would pop
popcorn, my brother, sisters, mother,
and I, and watch Dad on TV shows one

after another. Tiffany, my mom's daughter from another relationship, was also with us. We popped popcorn and watched movies with Floyd (stepfather) as well.

When we got back, I told my father I wanted to stay with my mother. He told me that I would understand when I became older that it was best for me to remain at home with him. I was going to see things that would change my life. He hugged me and told me to go to my room.

The next day it was back to normal playing with my new found friends. One person who became a really good friend of mine was Dwayne Williams. He is still a good friend of mine to this day.

Our cousins, Robbin and Lynda Camper, would continually come over to the house and play with my sisters. Also, our cousins, Melvin and Byron Thompson, would come over and play with my brother and I. We would have pillow fights.

I wasn't spending much time with my father. I not only wanted to live with him, but I wanted to go places with him and have father and son moments. Well, that didn't happen. I picked up a habit that was very bad for my health. I started smoking like my mother and father. I was only 14 at the time.

My father called us to let us know he was going to appear on television, and we wished him good luck on the show. It was so much fun to see him on there doing what he loved. We all loved him so. Some of our favorite places to go and eat were White's Shrimp restaurant and Italian Fiesta Pizzeria. Nothing was too good for his children. He always treated us fairly.

When my father made the money from his songs, he bought my grandpa a new car, and we were all so happy. I miss Grandpa so much!

At this time, I was going to be in the talent show at school. The group was called The Boyz. The members were Dwayne Williams, Verdell Douglas and myself. We were going to sing The Miracle's new song, *Do It Baby*. We were so cool. You couldn't tell us anything. We were "the bomb."

One day on my way home from school, I stopped at the store. Then my so-called friend, Jerome, puts a gun to my side and had me follow him into an alley. Once we got there, he stole my money! Can you believe this? Then he told me if I tell anyone that he would kill me. I didn't say anything for a month. When I did, he denied it. I told my parents, and they said I should have told them at the time. He was never punished for what he did. This guy was still in my class for the whole year of eighth grade.

But I'll never forget towards the end of the school year, Jerome and Michael were going to try to have an altercation with me. It wasn't enough that Jerome had robbed me at gunpoint earlier in the school year, and now here he was bothering me again. This time he had a friend with him. Well, my brother said not this time. When he confronted them, they backed down. Eugene Jr. had a way with words and would get his point across every time. They never said anything else to me.

There was no cable television or computers like there are today. My brother and I would get the mail every day to see if any magazines or records came. We were crazy about music and would play them every day. I was in a band by now, and I would go down the street to Kenny and Michael Avery's house and play.

My sisters were dancing in recitals, and we were going to have a little sister. This was great. When Gena came into this world, all of us were happy about our little sister. It was like a flower had blossomed in our home. I was always smiling, and I always got along with everyone. However, my brother and I had some fights just like brothers do. Other than that though, all was well.

I remember when we were going to see my father perform at the T.W.O. Theater. The day before the performance, my sisters and I were talking about how we could go on stage with my dad. You see, Marshall had a part in the act where he called up some dancers, and they would just start dancing. So all day, we talked about what we were going to wear and what dance we were going to do when he called our name. Once we finished our lengthy conversation, we finally got some sleep. That morning came and we were super excited, so we went outside and played in the front. We couldn't go too far from the house because Dad didn't want us going anywhere without supervision.

However, he made our lives very comfortable by providing us with whatever we needed and all our hearts' desires like pinball machines, pool tables, ping pong tables and an Atari video system with games. We were one of the first ones on the block to own one and that made us feel very privileged. Dad really made us feel special.

So we played outside that day until it was time to shower and get ready for the show that night. Whenever Dad played in town, we mostly went to see him. We loved to go and he loved taking us. He was not a "show boat" type of individual. He wanted everyone to recognize that he had kids and who they were. We pulled

up in the Cadillac every time we went
to a show, or Dad used a limo
service.

Our father took four hours or
more to get ready, so we got in the
shower early and went downstairs to
listen to music until he got dressed.
We were practicing our dance moves
for when we would get called on
stage. My brother and I were also
going over all the LPs that came in
during the month. We got a kick out
of checking out the new music on the
label.

The phone kept on ringing and
that's when we knew it was almost
time to go. You see my dad took
forever to get to a show. They would
be calling him repeatedly to urge him
to get ready faster. But that didn't
bother him. He made sure he was "neat
as a pin" before he came out of the
house.

Jackie told us to come upstairs, so we knew it was time. I had my lucky socks on and my high heel shoes. I just knew I was cool. We got in the car and it was on! When we got there, the people were lined up around the theater, and we went to the backstage area and then to our seats. The show began and we were having loads of fun! The Soul Train dancers back then were Jody Watley, and "Mr. Pop Lock" himself, Jeffrey Daniel from Shalamar. They really got down!

When The Chi-Lites came on stage, the crowd went nuts! I loved to see my father on stage. So many people loved him. My father in lights, shining so bright for all to see. He was my dad and I loved him no matter what he did - whether he sang or just said good morning to me when I woke up.

My father was not a "touchy" type of person. You see kids and parents holding one another, but my father was not that way. Nevertheless, I still knew he loved me. He didn't spend his money or what he would call "dough" on anyone he didn't care about.

He was on stage just dancing and singing when the part came up, and I stopped daydreaming. Marshall said, "Come up on the stage if you got what it takes!" I jumped up there with my sisters and we got down! I never conceived of it as being a "break" for me. I simply wanted some time with my father and that's what I got. Every chance I got I jumped on stage with him.

Now at this time, I had started doing something I saw on TV. A woman that wanted to lose weight was sticking her finger down her throat so she would not gain weight. So I thought that it would be a good idea for me to try this. I did this for about six months to a year. I would eat my dinner, then go straight to the bathroom and stick my finger down my throat and throw up all my food. I liked the way I looked, and I didn't want to get fat. I have seen people that were fat, and I could not live that way. Later on in life, I found out that this was an eating disorder called bulimia. I was so glad that I stopped on my own.

In 1976, I woke up one morning to my friends telling me that my dad was on the front of the Chicago Sun-Times newspaper for tax evasion. Now at the time, we were attending school at Our Lady of Peace. While we were at school, kids would tease me about it, and I was going to fight them about the matter.

On the way home, a car was following us. As my sisters and brother and I were talking about it, suddenly my father came out of nowhere and told us to get in the car. We were so scared, so we jumped in. Dad did not say anything, so we didn't say anything either. However, these troubled times were soon behind us.

Boy, every time I would see Dad on that stage singing and just doing his thing, it made me almost gasp for air! I mean, he would set off a certain joy in me, and just like I saw him as a child for the first time, it continued on each time. My dad sounded the same on stage as at home, but the lights on him made it even more spectacular and breathtaking to watch. I imagine because of the excitement of it all, that gave Dad the enthusiasm to sing with the utmost clarity and confidence. You always take the time after they are gone to think about the most personable details.

The show would be ready to start and the crowd would be chanting "Chi-Lites, Chi-Lites," and the room would go dark and just for a moment you feel such exhilaration, and then you hear the music. They had such showmanship as you heard the horns shout, and so they would start to rapidly go on for five or ten minutes showing the people what was in store. Then the lights would come on! You see, it's all about the lights. So now you have the music and the lights at this point.

I'm thinking about when I was in the first grade drawing my dad singing on television, and my teacher, Ms. Red, would catch me and now here he is. So they would run out with some of the most lavish and stylish ensembles. Their outfits were white, so every time the lights changed colors, the suits did as well.

You see, The Chi-Lites were by no means shy, and this was their come out party. Red had a tight feel with his steps as he would not move out of sync one bit. With his shoulder staying right by his neck so as to not show it, knowing that he is the bass singer and their expression is always theatrical.

Then you had Squirrel with his silky smooth moves almost like he had skates on doing the crazy legs as he moved from side to side only from the waist down as his body moved up and down.

Then you had Marshall as he would turn around from time to time. Being the band director, he would at times throw his hands up to control the tempo level as well as changes and accents, and at the same time, communicate with the crowd.

Last but not least, Dad with his straight arm going forward and back again, keeping his hand almost flat at times going in and out of steps only to belt out that voice as he moves to a side view.

This was a live performance by The Chi-Lites. For years, I watched them on live shows, television, and rehearsals. An unbelievable sight to see!

Dad loved performing, but not more than creating the "forever" track. "The Doctor", they called him, or "Genie Boy" or "One Track" all are nicknames he earned because of his innovative style.

During the middle of the show, I would run up on the stage and dance for a moment. Dad looked so happy, and I had the time of my life! Afterwards, we would go backstage and hang out with whoever had performed on the show, and then it was out to dinner with the family. My dad loved the lights, but he knew how much hard work it took to receive the fame, and of course, the fortune. He was by far a perfectionist.

We always knew my father would come back for us. He could have made other decisions, but he chose to give us all what he had which means so much to me.

I give a lot of credit to the children of entertainers, for the time they lack from their father or mother manifests in many different ways. I've found out that it is hard for people to accept this fact; most are in denial of the matter. The entertainer knows they are not there, but they lack the knowledge to make up for that and there really is no way to do that. As a child, whatever happens to you, it is elevated good or bad. For example, I broke my arm at school and they said there goes "a broken record."

We sometimes caught ourselves in a whirlwind trying to get our dad's attention. It was almost impossible with his schedule. Sometimes he was there, but he wasn't, "you dig" as he would say.

We had a lot of events that Dad was not able to come to. Even though we as children knew he was on the road, we just wanted our father to see us shine so we could feel the confidence we needed. We knew when Dad would come home, but we didn't really get a chance to talk to him, and when we did, we told him so much I don't think he could gather it all. But he in his own way made us feel special, and never did he leave us without.

If he had something, we were invited to it as well. We loved sitting in his studio and just watching him just go at it. Dad was always dealing with sounds. When he watched television, he got into grooves just sitting there. I've watched him pick up the guitar and just start going at it still checking out the tube.

You know, if your head turns back one time that's all it takes so to speak. You are grown and life has your number, and you automatically get a ticket whether you like it or not. Looking back to that special time, we had it all, and I thank him for just loving us and showing us the way. Even if it took some of us longer than others, he never gave up on telling us what we needed to hear.

There was a time I was not doing so well in school and not passing to the next grade. Some of my friends and I did not pass to the eighth grade. We were in my sister Michelle's seventh grade class for a week. The next thing I knew, I was told to go to the eighth grade room.

I was pushed through to the next grade.

I don't know what they did, but if I had a learning disability, it should have been addressed at that time. Throughout my school years from kindergarten to fourth grade, I was always having problems with putting things together. When the teachers would send me home with a note about it, my grandparents did the best they could do. My real parents were not there to help me. My mother should have been there for me. I was just another child with no pre-school training like a lot of the kids in my area.

Some kids have the confidence to overcome those types of obstacles. Sadly, I wasn't one of those kids. My brother handled it better than me.

I knew I had a problem when I first met my soon-to-be stepmother, Jackie. She would come over and try to teach me how to say beautiful. I could not say that word for nothing in the world.

At this time, I read an article in the Jet Magazine "People are Talking About" that said Dad was leaving the group for greener pastures or money so to speak, but this was not true. My father wanted to spend more time with his family and producing would do this. He would not have to tour, and this would give him the time he needed with us and it proved true. Dad said, "No way I could be with someone for sixteen years and leave for money." Warner Brothers signed Dad as well as Hank Williams Jr. to the Warner-Curb label for a more country-pop direction.

We were so happy when Dad got with Warner Brothers; they were a class act! Champaign every Christmas, all of Warner's albums, and we were into the artists at that time - Fleetwood Mac, Prince, and many others on the label. There was a trip to California where we hung out in Bel-Air and Burbank, and so Dad was spending more time with us. This was the best time for us kids. We did a lot of barbeques, and we would watch movies in the basement. Dad would light the fireplace in the winter on those cold nights in Chicago (known to most as "The Windy City").

EUGENE RECORD WITH WB

WARNER BROTHERS

Chapter Six

After writing for over twenty musical acts, it was time for my father to move on. One thing about my dad, when he would decide to do something, his mind was made up for real.

The school year was here for me, and it was the 200th anniversary of the adoption of the Declaration of Independence. They called it the United States Bicentennial, so red, white, and blue was the colors for the graduation. The class went to see the famous arch in St. Louis which had recently been built. Of course, I took the valedictorian out to the ball.

141

After graduation night, we went out to dinner with my family and had a good time. I was young at the time and was just happy to be out of school for the year.

Dad spent time at Paul Serrano Recording Studios and Streeterville Recording Studios in Chicago when he recorded the Eugene Record album. We spent a lot of time as children in the recording studio and learned from some of the best. We also spent time in Paragon Recording Studios. We knew almost everyone there because we frequented this studio for years.

Dad had his new publishing company, Angelshell, named after my two sisters, Michelle and Angela. Dad had the background vocals by Barbara Acklin and Wales Wallace, and they did a great job with Dad. My good friend, Louis Satterfield, played horns on the work along with Willie Henderson. They were a couple of well-seasoned musicians added to the

mix to make it just right. These
artists are just some of the "Greats"
that the world has been sampling for
years. Quinton Joseph brought his
"hard funk foot" with him on drums,
and Tom Tom Washington was arranging
the horns.

These irresistible love songs
are some of Dad's best works. One fan
wrote that the music on this LP is
intoxicating, breathtaking and
captivating. We were teens when it
came out, and we loved it then and
even now. A song from the album that
gets me every time is *Here Comes the
Sun*. It's a special way of saying
when the sun comes out, so does your
smile, and oh how he jazzed it up for
a great feel!

Phil Upchurch also performed on
this project. I mean, Dad went and
got the "real boys," so he was not
just playing around. *Overdose of Joy*
plays out as the man suffering from
too much happiness, and it is told in

such a soothing, musical way. These love-driven songs on this LP are what you need if you want to just chill with your companion and have a little wine and say what you feel.

The way Dad lays out the remake, *Putting It Down (To The Way I Feel About You),* written by Ken Gold, sounds like it was written for him. The arrangements on this song are amazing as the master piano starts and the music climbs the ladder to his voice. Dad came in at a smooth tone that is just right. Dad had that falsetto together, but he twisted a little natural in with it. Then right when you think you heard it all, he brings that Chi-Lite run vocal in such a subtle way as he vamps it out. I put this album on when I'm chilling at home.

After Dad recorded his *Laying Beside You* album for promotion, we went up north to the skating rink for him to skate and perform his song, and it was a blast seeing Dad glide across the floor. I had never in all my years seen how smooth he was. He sang his song with such ease using his cordless microphone, something you didn't see too often during this period of time. I didn't know that they were still pressing up eight track tapes in 1977, but they did. I was surprised that Warner Music Japan pressed up the compact disc and is still successfully selling them. Online right now the CD sells for $50 in the U.S. This music was also sampled by De La Soul's *He Comes* and Fusion Unlimited's *The Sun.*

In 1977, Dad took us to California for the summer. One of my dreams was to meet the Brothers Johnson when we got to California. I guess what they say about fate is true because when we got there, who's at the airport live and in color, the Brothers Johnson. I was outdone. You see, I had been playing bass for a long time. Louis Johnson is one of the pioneers of bass guitar.

My father was there on business, but he wanted his kids to have a wonderful time. Dad made our month there extraordinary. I loved the time my father spent with us. We swam and did other fun things together.

We stayed at Herbert Hoover's grandchildren's house in Bel Air. We ate with The Gap Band during our stay there.

Tom Tom Washington took me to see Earth, Wind & Fire's studio to watch them record. They recorded their best LP all and all. This was like a dream come true for me because the sound they had was my favorite. I always loved the group. The horns were the best in the band, and the arrangements Tom did were unforgettable. I was 14 years old, but I knew at that moment what I wanted to do with my life.

A short time later, while we were there, we learned about the King of Rock 'n Roll, Elvis Presley's death. I remember being at the pool when they said Elvis had died. My brother and I knew how to swim very well because we had gone to the Y.M.C.A. every summer when we lived with our grandparents.

We went across the street to the Ohio Players' studio and hung out. I had a lot of fun that day. Bel Air was a very enjoyable place. Later on in life, I told everyone I was the first Fresh Prince of Bel Air.

Our cousins stayed in California as well, and we had so much fun that summer. The Hoover house had six or seven bedrooms and a maid quarter. I wanted to stay there forever. We were so very happy at this time. Money did not seem to be a problem at all. My dad had some business there because I didn't see him as much as I wanted to, but I was still happy. When we did go somewhere, they would take pictures of us.

We also hung out with Smokey Robinson. Claudette, Smokey's wife, is my stepmom's very good friend to this day.

In my wildest imagination, I could not believe I was put in a position to tell a story that needed to be told. All the blessings that I'd been given was so overwhelming that I just held on tight and began to enjoy them. My father always told me to work hard. When I say work hard, I mean he showed us. It's funny when you tell someone something without saying a word. It sticks with you. Anyway, back to the story. When we got back to Chicago, we pulled up in the limo and got out. All the kids in the neighborhood gathered around to see us, and I felt good and refreshed. I wanted to start a new chapter in my life by refraining from such activities like hanging out, but my friends were right there. Peer pressure is like the mother of all pressure. My friends would say things like, "You think you too good for us now, huh? We aren't your boys anymore." After a day or so of that, I gave in and started right back.

At this time, my girlfriend said she was having a baby, and I was speechless. We started having problems. I didn't know what to do. Later, we separated.

I recall being at home one day and my father was out of town on tour or recording. My sisters were at Nana's (Amanda Sutton, Jackie's mom) house. I don't remember where my brother was, but I think Jackie asked him did he want to go and see The Temptations and he said no. I was the only one left that had nothing to do; I loved to see live music. I guess that is my number one thing with music. So Jackie asked me and I accepted. Afterwards, Jackie went to get dressed and I did as well.

We left and went to the hotel where Melvin of The Temptations was at. I was so excited because I loved the group so much, and for Jackie to know him personally, that was so impressive to me. Melvin looked at me and said with that low, low voice of his, "Who is this little fella?" I tried to tell him my name, but it didn't come out. Jackie told him my name was Brian, then he said, "Glad to meet you, Brian. Are you ready to go?" Then I said yes. We went down the back part of the hotel, and a big, long, black limousine pulled up and the door opened. I jumped in, but I only made it half way. I felt something pulling me back out; it was Melvin. He looked at me and said, "Ladies first, Brian." I was embarrassed a little only because it was Melvin, but that stuck with me for the rest of my life. Every time after that, I made sure it was always ladies first, whatever I did. Even now, I am thankful that he showed me the way it is supposed to be done.

Getting back to the limo, we drove to the show and pulled up to the backstage area, and we got out and made our way to the dressing rooms. Melvin went to get dressed, and Jackie and I went to get our seats. The anticipation of the show was hard to handle. The music started and The Temptations hit the stage. It was magnificent! They sang all the songs I loved. I was mostly noticing Melvin. He was really getting down. The other guys did OK as well.

After the show, we went backstage. I was accustomed to going backstage with the stars with my father. After I met all The Temptations, we got ready to go. We left in the big black limousine, and then we went to the hotel where the car was. Jackie and I went home. The very next day, Melvin, his friend, and son visited us. Jackie started cooking fried chicken, and Melvin, his son and I went downstairs in the basement. We watched television and he began talking to me.

He asked me what I was going to be when I grew up. I told him I wanted to write and compose music like my dad. He then asked me was there something else I wanted to be as well. I told him I loved to draw. He told me no matter what I wanted to do, make sure you love what you are doing because you will be doing it for the rest of your life. Afterwards, I told him that I have always wanted to perform, not record, but just perform all my life. I loved the energy that you get when you get on stage. He then told me that I need to do just that because it is what I love.

At the end of the day, the limo came back to pick up Melvin, and we said our goodbyes. I never saw Melvin again in person, but I will never forget how well he treated me and how graceful he was. He was someone who was very special to me.

My brother was back from college because of the death of our grandfather. Grandpa was shoveling the snow and suffered a major heart attack and died upon arriving at the hospital. My father and family was devastated. If this wasn't enough, my brother ingested some alcohol with his medication and had a reaction. He went through something drastic while he was away in college. He was never quite the same for years afterwards. My father told me to hold my brother as we put him in the car together. I was so scared at the time. I thought I was going to lose him. I had lost one brother and one sister already in this world. I was so happy that he was going to be OK.

After Dad had mourned and some time had passed, Dad got back to recording. As I'm watching Dad, the song, *Trying to Get to You*, plays and Dad and Louis Satterfield played bass guitar. I loved the choice of musicians on this work. We liked the promotion as well for this LP.

The song, *Come to My Party*, is real special because Tom Washington co-composed this song with my dad and that didn't occur too much. It is a terrific commercial song, and 1 love the background vocals and arrangements Tom puts in this work of artistry. I was there when they worked on the song, and it was fascinating the way Tom could take over when he was called. He knew just what to do. The aura in the room when these masters were at work was mind-blowing!

See, musicians from any era know good work when they hear it. It takes a person with a special finesse to have the ability to grab that sample out the air. The same "rule of thumb" applies with the talent that is found now. Old or new, you either got it or you don't. Writing is a gift from God.

The song, *Welcome to My Fantasy,* is a one time writing collaboration of Dad and newcomer, Barbara Bailey, who delivered a unique dressed up, and high party background vocal that celebrates this adventure. There was likewise a top of the line strong production by Andraé Crouch as well.

At this time, all of the children were in high school except for Gena, so we missed a lot of the recording of the last album. So when we heard it for the first time, we thought it had a little different sound, but we thought it was great work. This album was mixed in Hollywood, so Dad went out there to take care of business.

Michael Davis, another "Great," played horns on this track. Dad continued to play the synthesizers on the album, and of course, the master, Mr. Willie Henderson, was on strings. Louis Minter, also one of Dad's horn players that traveled with him throughout his years as an entertainer, joined the project as well. Patrick Henderson produced the project with Dad, a sound that has never been duplicated.

Coming through the 1970's took its toll on us. Dad had some experiences after the struggle in the 1960's with his family and then the struggle with the record companies. Dad went from having a number one hit on television, radio, movie theaters, and commercials, to being in court, signing with Warner Brothers Records, and only three years later returning to The Chi-Lites for a last run with "The Boys."

My brother, Junior, started talking about joining the army, and my dad didn't like the idea. However, once my brother makes his mind up about doing something, there's no talking him out of it. He probably gets that from Dad.

My brother and I had never been away from each other. This was going to be a huge step for him, but I believed it was going to be for his own good. He was going to the army to serve his country.

EUGENE WITH CHI-SOUND

CHI-SOUND

Chapter Seven

No matter how much recording Dad had to do, he always seemed to have us there when the strings and horns were being laid. This was my favorite part of the session other than the mix down; it seemed everyone was in a very good mood. When I was at Universal Studios in Chicago on Rush Street, this was my all time favorite because when they were recording in Studio A, I was in Studio B jamming and having a good time with Brian Davis (Carl Davis' son). We would also spend time in the editing room.

Dad worked real hard at the studio; this was after he worked tireless nights at home with the

159

track. A masterpiece took a certain amount of hours. Some songs exceeded hundreds of hours if you take into consideration the time and effort that went into preparing, the gathering of musicians, and them getting it just right. It wasn't like the digital correction software they have now, but sometimes fast isn't good.

Also, I can tell real strings from the keyboards. I guess that's what you get being around the real thing. I know some say a keyboard is nothing but a sound chip, but when Dad used them he wanted both; he said he couldn't be fooled and he needed the real thing. As I check out Dad's tracks, I can tell what is real, and I love the finished product that is produced. You can only play on the keyboard what was put in and that's all; you can make a percussion sound on it, but it stops there. Great musicians record instruments in those keyboards, and without them, there would be no sound.

I really appreciate my father spending time with us teaching us that our music is special whether someone buys it or not. Some music never takes off the whole lifetime of that musician, but somewhere down the line, it gets noticed, and if the musician had given up, his work wouldn't matter.

The 1980's brought four albums from The Chi-Lites and one from The Dells that Dad had "his foot" in, and it had another whole new sound for them. Dad had just finished the work with Warner Brothers though it did not sell as rapidly as he wanted. Dad told me long ago that some works don't take off right away. Those songs now are steadily selling and will continue just like any good music does.

The sound kind of had a little "Eugene Record identity" in there more than before. "Eugene the producer" was always there, but now this new sound was intriguing enough for the fans to start listening again. The Chi-Lites' *Heavenly Body* featured Gene Record, and he did something he usually would not do. He added his voice several times on the background to make a new sound. This sound I call "Chi-Sound." This made the comeback with Carl Davis' label, and with Dad's writing "knack," the "aura" happened once again and got some renewed attention.

Dad had started to repeat a style from his earlier years. The first two albums with The Chi-Lites, he had that island twist like in the *Are You My Woman* track. That's why those two albums were my favorite. It had a young hip hop feel to it way back then, and he brought it back in the 1980's at Chi-Sound. The song, *Give Me a Dream,* speaks of how we all feel overwhelmed at times dealing with reality. The closer, *Super Mad About You Baby*, was Dad simply saying he was in love, and it was super!

The family was happy for Dad at the time. He made it back from Cali, and we were happy he had found his way back to the group with a new sound. He started writing with more people. Dad started collaborating with family members. He wrote songs with his wife, Jackie, his brother, LP, and me (Brian). Dad was trying new things in the eighties and it felt good.

We would be at the house for Christmas every year and hang out with the family. Dad always seemed so happy with his family, and he treasured the time. His music was evolving, and the samples were on their way. The next album was soon to arrive, but we as children had heard the next set of songs already it seemed. When he put the album out, we knew it front to back and the next one as well.

Dad had been working with The Dells' new album after the mix up of all record labels in the early 1970's. The Chicago acts seem to come back home, so Dad went back to work with The Dells on the album, *I Touched a Dream*. That's when I got a chance to really get to know this talented bunch of guys. The vocals were irreplaceable; the sound of their voices blended so well together.

Day in and day out, my friend, Dwayne, and I hung out at the studio seeing The Dells put finishing work to the album. We learned a lot from the fifty plus musicians that was there, and what it was about back then was all that power you got rolled into one product. People at present still can't get enough of those works because still to this day it is selling.

After that, we celebrated with the label, and it was time for Dad to tour again. We were so happy for him, but he had to go back on the road. We did not look forward to him leaving.

After a while, we got a call from home. I can imagine my father's feelings when he and all of us heard that my grandmother was sick. So we went to be with her at the hospital. After some time, Gran died. She not only raised my father and his siblings, but a hand full of grandchildren including my brother and I. My grandmother had worked at the post office 22½ years.

Our family felt a sort of pain like no other, you see, when Gran died. She was "the glue" that helped hold the family together, and now it was gone. Yes the family saw a lot of each other, but the obligation that everyone had to visit Gran was gone. I saw my family, but not all together.

It seemed for a time everyone went their own way. The family seemed so hurt and they found ways to hurt one another, and at the same time, the kids suffered. She taught us to come together and help one another, but that went out the window. I have never ever seen the whole family together not even at funerals. Time seems to take its toll on you as you say goodbye to loved ones like Gran.

Afterwards, Dad didn't do much. This actually got Dad to start spending a lot more time with family again. We talked about it a little, but he would shy away from it whenever I brought it up. So I just kind of let it go. But I could see a change in him even in the next music he would put out.

When he got back to the studio, he was himself. *You and I* came out and just like always, my brother and I were discussing the "ins and outs" of it all and listening to the songs to see where he was going with it.

First, on the next album, Dad wore black, and I took that as a sure enough sign that was out of respect for his mother. Dad's hand was stretched out so elegantly. He even cut his hair down. I liked Dad's new look. It made him look more distinguished.

The song we all loved was *Hot on a Thing (Called Love)*. We all watched Dad perform that on Soul Train. It was on fire back then, but I still hear the song playing in clubs and on the radio, and it makes good dance music.

After that tour and Christmas had gone by, we found out that Red was not going to be with the group once again. He was going through some tough times, and as kids, we pretty much brushed it off. You know we didn't know too much about the business side of the group, only what we were told or what we could hear. My sister, Michelle, usually had the 411 on everything, but even she was low key about Red. We thought the group was going to get another member, but the group said they would just go with the three.

I saw them play with just the three and they held their own, and in the studio, Barbara laid some background on some of the hottest tracks The Chi-Lites did.

Dad and his brother were touring together, and I thought it was a blast seeing those brothers hanging out together.

Los Angeles Recording Company (LARC) worked on the next project. Dad worked with Recording Engineer Danny Leake. Danny has worked with some of the top recording artists in the world and is working with Stevie Wonder as I write this book. Also Ronald Scott, one of Dad's close friends, spent a lot of nights in the studio recording with Dad. He is a pastor now, and he is still recording and remains close to the family.

Changing for You was a nice stepper's cut which was really good for The Chi-Lites. I thought it was just what they needed. *Bottom's Up* was hot and I think maybe they were thinking The Gap Band, and this is The Chi-Lites' turn for "new school." The group was going from love songs to dance and party, and the next would continue to be that same change. However, he enjoyed writing and he tried a little dance music. He had already had a hit dance single in Europe called *Magnetism*. The song, *Bad Motor Scooter*, I thought would have been in an animation movie by now since it fits the profile.

Steppin' Out was with the same head guy, Joe Isgro, who had LARC and established a second label, Private I Records distributed through Columbia Records. This one was very hot and I was surprised it did not do better, but it is a classic today. Arranged by Dad and Sonny Sanders, it has that same smooth glide that The Chi-Lites are known for, and with Dad as producer, he gets the job done.

Using the S-50 and D-50 Roland, Dad creates a dance sound that today still hits you in the face in *Stop What You're Doing*. I was in the

170

studio at this time every day with the group. We stayed in there for days. I really liked what I heard. It's the most time Dad had used a synthesizer to capture the sound. He had done everything on guitar before.

Gimme Whatcha Got, what can I say, written by Dad and his brother, Leslie Paul Record. Seeing them together every day just touched my heart, and it was something that did not go on until this time in Dad's life. Dad started to get closer to his siblings after his parents were gone, and it made me feel good to see them writing together.

You see, everything was changing. The strings and timpani had stopped, and we started using the computers which took something away from it all. Yes, I loved the folk and dance tunes, but when you put them all together - the strings, the voices, and the arrangements - it's clear you have something not only spectacular, but irreplaceable to the ear. That's what makes the samples so strong that you want to take an album of maybe fifty or more musicians and sample that with your electronic music together. It gives off a sound that will make people continue to buy that product, and they won't know why it's got them hooked like that.

I remember when Dad was with Chi-Sound Records. That was the last part of his recording career as an R&B artist. The studio was on the north side of Chicago. I was there almost every day with The Chi-Lites recording. It was located near the famous Rush Street.

At night, I would go and hang out with my longtime friend, Dwayne. We would have a blast. I would put my sunglasses on, and then I thought I was on top of the world. Let me get back to the studio recording and learning from the best. We would hang out with the stars as they came in. Then we would sit and learn.

When I was at the house with Dad, we were always recording. He told me that he always recorded because he said, "If it isn't broke, don't fix it. This is what I love to do." One day, he told me that his children inspired him to want to work hard when he was young between the ages of 20 and 30. I wanted the best for my kids, so I worked really hard as well.

I remember there was a time when I was going to open up live for a show with The Chi-Lites for the first time ever. This occurred at the Copper Box on the south side of Chicago. Starring on the show was the S.O.S. Band, Next Movement, The Chi-Lites, and my group, Prime Time. We had been in the local newspaper throughout the year and had made a name for ourselves in the city.

After practicing for a full week, it was time to make this happen. I found out at the last minute that we were going to open for the show.

There were a lot of people in the crowd that were famous. This was it! What the people didn't know was that we were a black rock band, and all the other groups on the show were R&B.

Well, we hit with a hard rock opener and the crowd went wild. I was jumping up and down like I was crazy similar to the group band, Kiss. I don't know if you have seen the band, Kiss. They are wild and so was I.

After the first song, the people just had their mouth opened. I don't think they were ready for a black rock band at this time. Our band kept performing for full crowds on the north side of Chicago for two years, and then we gave up on the group.

I was brought up around a wide variety of music. I have never loved one kind of music. That is why I loved performing because you can be who or what you want to be any night of the year. If you want to be a rock band tonight, you can. If you want to be an R&B band, you can. If you want to be a rapper, then you are a rapper that night.

Dad performed for what he thought was the last time with The Chi-Lites in the eighties, but it would not be his last.

Dad in the Home Studio

THE LIGHT

Chapter Eight

My dad called me and asked me to come over one day "out of the blue." When I went, he told me he had something for me and handed me a Bible. He told me he had found Jesus. I didn't know what to think of this until he started calling me and speaking to me about God.

My father had never just called me "out of the blue" like that talking about spiritual matters. He started telling me how much I needed to take a look at myself and my family and put God first, and make sure I pick the right religion so I'm not led astray.

During the 1990's, Dad found himself by continuously working on his songs, getting the house remodeled, and doing all the work that needed to be done around the house. But at this time, a different light was on the agenda for Dad. This light shined brighter than any on the earth, and no human being can construct the light that radiated from my father.

Dad worked a little bit differently than before. He got the call, gathered his music on faith, and started on the quest for greatness. People have yet to know the work that was put into the gospel music that he performed. It will go down in history as some of the most angelic multi tracking performances I have heard. Dad used the Bruce Swedien method they created long ago. Michael Jackson used it as well in the *Thriller* album.

I've only heard or felt the same when Michael sang songs about the world. Dad singing about Jesus sends chills through my body when I hear the songs from the *Let Him In* album.

Dad wanted to travel the world and see what his calling was all about, so he visited the Red Sea and recorded his experience and went in deep by living it. There is nothing like seeing for yourself the life that Jesus lived, giving account of his life, and writing his music from not just experience, but inspiration.

In Dad's mind's eye, he couldn't see past his younger years when he had all the painful experiences with the family. But now he had to search for that same feeling to get inspired, so he searched for that inspiration from different cities that would give him the words he needed. This is one of the reasons my eyes opened when I saw him searching.

Dad also continued to work on his new identity by being more open to conversation with the family as well as people in general. He became even more gentle and humble. People say they want to find out how God works; well he continues to show up at the right time and the right place. Dad showed that God is alive and he works through people.

Dad also talked to Robert Kelly at the house, and during this time, they attended the same church. Robert's first cousin, Blackie, would come along and that's how he met my youngest sister, Gena. They eventually fell in love, got married, and are happily ever after, a family with beautiful children. After that, the two families are now entwined and have two of the greatest songwriters to ever come out of Chicago.

Dad had told me that MC Hammer was going to put one of his songs on the album. At that point, I knew whatever song it was, it would sell because this was the age of sampling, and if you had the right tune, you had it made. MC Hammer remade *Have You Seen Her* at the right time. He did not sample it. The song was a classic for twenty years. Kids who had heard the song when it first came out were grown up by now. Since it was a classic, the next generation was familiar with the song as well. Music was changing and they wanted to hear what they came upon, so together you had two decades of this song and the new kids that would cling on to it from MC Hammer. He was on his way up, so he mixed the hip hop rap feel with old school rhythm and blues. A couple of artists tried it, but never went large. Dad sang the song about the lady he lost and could not find, but MC Hammer sang about a lady he never met and this was a genuine twist that was truly commercial.

Dad was presented with the 10 million sold Diamond award album CD plaque. This was a great accomplishment for Dad to move him in the direction he needed to go. With his mind focused on the Lord, he now had what he needed to take on the mission that God had for him. Funny how things work out, or is it the way God opens the windows for you?

So Dad continued to gather the songs for the family's future. Everything Dad did and the decisions he made was always for his family. His last works show that he was pointing his family in the best direction he knew.

After coming off tour with The Chi-Lites for a couple of years, Uncle Leslie got the bad news; the news no parent ever wants to hear.

Just like my mom and dad went through the pain of having their children taken from them at such an early age, I watched my uncle Leslie go through the pain of his son's death.

No matter what the circumstances is, it seems like people just don't get it. They see the pain you are going through, but don't really know the pain, that end of the world pain that you go through. When a child dies young, parents are not ready to go through the agony and hurt they must endure, not to mention at the same time trying to handle anything else that's going on, like bills, trouble, or just life in general. Put that together and you have chaos.

Then you have someone that doesn't know why you're acting a certain way, and they say you must be crazy or something. No, he's going through something you have yet to go through, but everyone's time comes

183

and this is a part of life. Oh, you'll get it eventually. The reason this plays such a significant role in my father's life is because Dad watched his only brother lose sight of his life at this point.

No matter what anyone said, he had a special relationship with his brother that no one could come between like my brother and I. We talk about things that you can't imagine from twenty years ago to yesterday; it keeps us where we should be with one another. We both know the truth; we can't fool one another at all. My brother lost his stepson he helped raise to street violence; he was an innocent bystander. The love he had for that child was felt two thousand miles away. I was not in pain for just the loss of the child, but for my best friend, my brother, Eugene Jr.

Dad's only brother had only two sons, Randolph and Alexander. One of them died in 1990. Dad spent some time with Leslie after Randolph Record, who was a DJ in Munich, Germany, passed. He was only 21 years of age at the time of his death.

After this, Dad for the first time talked to me about my brother, Vincent, and how the loss of Randy reminded him of his loss long ago. I was somewhat surprised that he mentioned that to me. He told me when he had his third son, he thought he had a singing group in the making and to see his three boys together would have been great. The pain his brother was going through must have been unexplainable and that no one should have to lose a child to this world.

Randy nearly grew up in our house because he didn't live that far away, so we saw each other every week. He was like a brother to me, and after that, Leslie was never the same, and my dad's relationship with his brother would never be the same.

You see, when someone loses a child, they are mad at the world, and they feel they have nowhere to turn and no one to blame. So they blame themselves, and the weight takes its toll on them. Dad consoled Leslie for weeks, and then he stayed away for some time. It is also timely how Dad now was in a position to fully counsel his brother with God's Word.

After traveling for some time now and recording the gospel project, Dad got a call. His sister, Patricia, had passed away. Just to remind you who she was to him, she was one of his first inspirations for playing music. She was an accomplished pianist. But what most people didn't know is she played gospel all her life.

You see, I told you before, when we were living with Gran, every Sunday morning Pat would wake me up to music. She would be playing gospel music. That piano was humming, but our family was Catholic, so gospel music was not embraced in our household. My father's music was R&B, or that was the name they gave it.

Dad recognized that she had it right all the time. She knew where the spirit would take this family all along, and he now was more determined to not only finish, but this added a new meaning to the project.

When Pat played that piano, it sounded like three people were playing it, no exaggeration. She really had something special. You see, after going through years of shock treatments and being in and out of mental health centers, she really did not have many places to go. She couldn't play the piano anywhere else, so she played that piano for dear life. You know what I mean?

She didn't know if she would have a chance to play again, so she played like it was the last time - like eating your last meal, like seeing your child for the last time, or like being in love, but having no one there to receive it. People don't know how that feels until they are faced with that, and then you know that it is time to walk the walk.

Dad talked to me about his sister and told me he thought about his sister everyday of his life. It was the one thing that he had no power over, but he knew she was going to be alright now that she went home and that she was with her mom and dad. This was so comforting to me, and when I hear that closing music of his, it reminds me of Pat in a way. It's like he put a little of her in it or she was already there, and I didn't notice it until then. It was strange how Dad died on July 22nd and Pat died on July 21st, so I woke up on my birthday and had just said goodbye to my favorite aunt, Patricia.

In 1995, Tommy, my stepmom's Dad, died and for some time Jackie grieved and so did the whole family. We used to call him Uncle Tommy, and he was a really gifted dancer. He was the founder of the Mayfair Academy of Fine Arts on the south side of Chicago. From what I know, Tommy and Dad got along very well, and they had much respect for one another. Tommy shared the same stage with known dancers like Bill "Bo Jangles" Robinson, Cab Calloway, Duke Ellington and Nat King Cole.

Dad lost his number one writing partner, Barbara Acklin. She was the lady with the hooks. She could pick up that hook in a song, and their collaborations were unstoppable.

Barbara was the first relationship Dad had after his marriage with Mom. The fact that they had music in common helped Dad build a solid relationship with Barbara after his failed marriage and loss of his two children. It helped him mourn by writing and bringing out the pain he had gone through.

However, by Barbara being an artist herself, this made Dad think twice about continuing a long relationship with her. He was looking for someone to help him with his ready-made family.

Dad cherished the friendship he had with Barbara. Their great writing relationship started at the same time and was very successful. The songs she and Dad wrote always had the feelings of a man and a woman - what a man would say and how he and she would feel about love. I believe that years from now people will notice their songs even more than they do now. They have so much truthful meaning to them. Dad was finishing his gospel album around the time she died, and a new chapter in his life was about to unfold.

This song, *Mother of Love*, was written about my stepmom that really expresses who she is at heart. She married my father and took charge of four children, and when she had her daughter, she continued with five. With my father and herself, she was responsible for seven people in the household, and she cooked and cleaned as well as worked as a school teacher, something that not everyone can accomplish. When Dad talks about Mother Goose (who we know is a fictional character), "had all those kids and made sure they had what they needed," she pushed forward and made it happen. All these tasks were done, and when Dad came back from being on the road, he came back to a home of peace.

You have to work hard at this. You don't make it happen overnight. Of course, there are good and bad times, but you roll up your sleeves and you go with the punches until you see your children becoming what they are here for - to be respected and responsible adults. *Mother of Love* sure fits Jackie. She still makes sure that all her children and grandchildren have what they need in life to sustain them and is still teaching us this very day.

Here Comes the Sun lets you know when things don't go your way, you don't have to fight it. When you don't hear what you want, it doesn't mean it's over. Smile and think happy thoughts, and just don't stop there.

Realize that love is just around the corner. The next day will be brighter if you just have faith. The sun was Jackie's smile. She was not going to leave him, but he had to win her trust back, so he wrote an apology. The love they had for one another would never be broken. She endured one of the hardest jobs in America, the spouse of an entertainer.

For the first time, there was a family reunion, and Dad was there. I have never seen him so happy to be around his family, and having the family together was great. Of course, I cooked and the family had a good time at the reunion.

Dad played a few instruments. Of course, everyone knows he plays guitar, but Dad also played bass guitar and very well I may add. Dad played a little keyboard as well, whatever he needed to get the job done. When he wrote a song, he made sure the sounds he was looking for were on point. So if he needed a master of that particular instrument, he called whoever could get the job done.

Dad also played the congas; he did on stage as well. Percussions were Dad's main concern after he got the basics laid. He wanted the "island feel" to jar you when you hear the music just bouncing and you just have to move. That's the shake and bake that gets you to move your body, and the percussions just take you there. Dad also sometimes played the snare; he liked laying a special snare sound he was looking for.

Dad, for a little while, rode his bike, and a couple of times we rode together when we were younger. He had a blue 29-inch Fuji bike which my brother, Eugene Jr., still rides on occasion. Dad had black precision boot skates. Dad bought us some weights, and my brother, Junior, was on the weights all the time. I hit them but not as much, but bike riding I loved. I can remember going bike riding once, and we (Dad, my brother and I) stopped for ice cream. You always remember those days.

Dad liked to fire up the grill from time to time, and of course, he had to make everything right in the backyard. If you knew Dad, he had to make sure the scenery was looking perfect in order that nothing would be in the way of him doing the job. We enjoyed our family times together just like everyone does, and so did he. He was just a humble man at heart wanting the best life for his family, and he would stop at nothing to achieve that.

After years of raising his family, Dad was about to give away his daughter in marriage. This was his youngest, Gena, who for the most part, grew up in the house that Dad built. Since she was the youngest one, we all watched after her. Dad even wrote a song about her called *Little Girl*, and it is still one of my favorites. The wedding was a beautiful one, although I did not attend due to illness, but my siblings said it was wonderful and my little sister was not so little any more. Dad was happy for Gena – Dad, the Grandfather.

My Father in Lites

Dad's *Let Him In* CD Cover

LET HIM IN

Chapter Nine

It's the year 2000 and Dad has released his CD on his label, Evergreen Records, and he is continuing to give the family guidance and support. He has his 60th birthday party, and it is a good time in his life. The kids have spread around the states and live in various places. We would call and we would talk mainly about God and family. He gave me the job of editing his web music, and I was happy to do so.

It took him almost eight years to create that work, and Dad mostly had something to do with every sound. If he didn't play it, he knew what and who he wanted and who could give him the sound he was looking for. With arrangements from Sonny Sanders, boy this is some special work!

It starts with *Let Him In*, a song that shows off Dad's famous falsetto chorus and harmonic voices with his natural voice leading, that talk voice that was meaningful in all his rap intros. I mean, all this in a super arrangement that is a magnificent hit! At the end, it slows down just enough so you can hear the timpani as the window of blessing comes down from heaven. That is what I hear.

The next song is *There Will Never be any Peace (Until God is Seated at the Conference Table)*. It starts with the kettle drums coming in as to introduce a king or someone in top rank to then give a message that is very clear. Dad wrote this song long ago with The Chi-Lites, and of course, Fantasia borrowed it for *Baby Momma*. Dad was always writing about love and justice, and this classic is great.

The next in line is *Never Been Satisfied*, a testimonial by my father as this horn topped start to finish as he saw how God was steering him into righteousness, so he followed through seeing the light. He praises him as the bridge goes and finds Jesus, and then he gives praise as his famous falsetto goes through. He testifies as the vamp closes, "Never Been Satisfied."

The next song has one of the best multi-malts of angelic voices that Dad is so famous for that is truly an *Instrument of Peace*. If this intro does not touch you there is something wrong. His lead voice sings, "Where there is any problem we will utter the name of God and spread love everywhere until the day of the

Lord." As his natural is used more than he ever did, I believe that is telling how serious one is in what they are saying.

The next song is *Just Pray*. Dad changed this song in the middle of getting the call from the Lord Jesus or an angel. This song was *Just Push Play*, and when the song comes in with this sharp flute and smooth stepper's feeling, you could just drive or just sit and get this testimony saying "just pray" in the name of Jesus, and he challenges you to do so and to see a change. This is one of Dad's greatest works. He played a lot of the instrumentation on this piece.

The next song, *Fresh Fire*, has some of the sharpest arrangements. The harp sounds and the live feelings and the convictions of his soul that he gives through this song, you really appreciate the praise from Dad and it is unbelievable! This song speaks with horns and instruments in order to wake up those asleep at the wheel of life just before it goes down so to speak.

Then next comes one of the strongest compositions on the CD, *One Voice*. The board in the intro is a smooth run of notes that fit so well with the voice that from the start, let's everyone know where it is going only to slap you into reality and then it's here. The message is very well put together and again, that famous falsetto voice we have come to know from Dad steps out to testify. See, that's one thing that makes it so special is hearing that voice we love testifying forever. Now that's special! It has that "Chi-Lite feel run" that I love and he did it for the Lord which makes me feel that it is forever!

The next song on the CD is *I'm Gonna Praise the Lord* which is

another upbeat song testifying that
his true showing is here right now,
and that natural again comes out to
show Dad's serious side that really
came out in his early years.

The next song is *He is the One.*
In this song, Dad uses his island
type of feel with the added conga
sound, but still shows his commitment
to serving the Lord Jesus Christ, and
then an instrumental of the steppin'
feel.

Such a marvelous work, and he
came and handed me copies of the CD
which I treasure to this day. On to
the radio stations we go.

Dad started promoting his album
from radio stations to making stops
at the record stores and got it
played, but people seemed surprised
about the news about Dad going
gospel. Still, we enjoyed it and knew
it was before its era, but in time,

we would find out what is there for certain.

Dad, for the first time, had begun to preach the word and also sing the good words of the Bible through his music, and it was special for all of us. He had waited so long for this moment, and he was so happy being in the radio booth with Gus. "Just like old times," they said. It was awe-inspiring to see how my little sister, Gena, was there managing Dad's affairs, and I had an entertainment newspaper that was there filming. Dad was so happy testifying on the radio and being able to play the music that he worked on so hard for his master!

Dad continued to work at home. He loved spending time at home with his wife, Jackie. He was certainly a homebody, and he loved having things the way they should be - clean, straight, even and right. He continued to write and compose during the week and spent time with his grandchildren. He really loved that.

My family and I hit the west coast and hung out with my brother, Eugene Jr., for about a year, and then I got the call from my brother. My dad had phoned him to give him the news that he had cancer. This hit the family with not just distress, but with anger. Most people don't react the right way about news like this, but is there even a right way to handle this?

My father, who took very good care of himself, had a dreadful disease. But everybody has a vice and my dad's was cigarettes. I mean, he came up in the age where smoking was cool. I love the old movies, and I see them smoking and it really looks kind of strange. But I myself took five years to quit smoking.

I was living in Vegas when I got the news, so we started packing to head home. My wife became ill as well, so the decision to come home was inevitable. When we got into Chicago, my sister, Angela, met my wife and I only to give us more bad news that my niece had passed. Starr was her name.

When we got to the hospital, my mother and father were there. My mom was on the third floor, and my dad was on the fifth floor. I visited Dad and Mom and we talked. He was strong leading by example. He told me, "Keep your word, it's all you have. Do what's right always and work on getting close with your children." It was so painful to talk to him just knowing he was entering a new journey. We and the family are just praying at this time to give our love and support to Dad and Mom.

Mom just held my hand and said, "I'm sorry." I didn't know why at the time she was saying this. But when you are sick in bed, you try to cover everything you can, so I held her and kissed her hand.

Dad wanted to sing back with the group after he found out, and in December of 2003, Dad reunited with the group to film the PBS Special, Superstars of Seventies Soul. Dad filmed in Vegas and invited my brother and me, but my wife and I were going through some family problems, so my brother went to the show.

Renowned Radio Personality Al Greer, who was a dear friend of my father's and who shared the same birthday with him, was trying to contact Dad for several days but to no avail. So he went over to his house to see him. Upon his arrival, he was asked to wait at the door.

After five minutes, Dad came to the top of the staircase, and they talked for a few minutes. At this time, Dad was very soft spoken but was happy to see him. That was the last moment he shared with his friend. As he left out the door, the nurse asked him who he was. He told her his name was Al Greer. She said to him, "You must be special because Eugene hardly gets out the bed for anyone." Al Greer and his brother have always been close to our family.

For days we sat by Dad's bed in my sister Gena's house and prayed with my father. He didn't talk very much, so I sat there for hours and just spoke to him. I spoke of anything that I could think of that I didn't say all these years. I told him, "I know it seems like we did not spend enough time together in this lifetime, but wherever you are going, I will be there soon. It may seem like a long time to others, but it will be just a moment to God," and I held his hand and he held my hand tight.

I left to go home with my family, and Michelle called that night to tell me he was gone. I was still in shock. My wife said I sat there for twenty minutes, but it only seemed like one. I called Uncle Marshall Thompson, who he loved very much, and we both cried together and we built each other up as well. I then talked to my brother, and we talked about old times with Dad.

You know, we were the men of the family, and we did a lot of "men stuff." It was always us three against the world, how we went shopping together and how we would work on the house together. This was work we did not want to do, but looking back on the times, we were able to have some time together. No matter what, it was our time.

The family was called together, and we held each other and conferred with each other on how we were to handle everything. Sitting there just thinking that the one person that knew me so well, the friend that I had and knew would never let me down or turn his back on me was gone. This was "the coldest day of my life." You know one of the most testing things about someone leaving you is when your friends try to console you because to me, it just seems to make the situation much worse.

I got there at the wake and I was walking up with my stepmom and Eugene Jr. slowly down the ramp just like before with my little sister, Darlene. One thing I left out is when my father sat down at the funeral with us and he started to cry with my mom. It made me even sadder to see him because one thing you understand when you are a child, you know about crying and you understand that this is what you do when you are unhappy or hurt.

So all the way to the box I walked only to find my dad is not with me. He is lying there sleeping. The best friend I ever had. Someone that never gave up on me even when I had was my father. He thought I was all right. Every time I saw him, he inspired me to take my time and whatever you love, do that because God has you here and no one else; this is between you and him.

After that spell, I sat down and started thinking about my father's legacy and what direction to go in. Dad loved writing and composing music, so I started there thinking to do what I could to promote my father, but this was only a thought.

My brother and I left to get our Dad a better tie. We drove to the store, walked around some, never coming down from our natural high and not really talking about what is going on. But we found the perfect one for him to go home with. So we raced back only to find photo hogs trying to get a picture of Dad. That really hurt.

We sat there and talked with each other and reminisced on the things we remembered about Dad and what he taught us. We talked about the fact that he would want us to come together and move forward and continue to learn and work hard. All these things he was good at, and we loved him for that. We also talked about how he sure would beat it home for some of his mom's homemade apple sauce and his father's biscuits with jelly.

The funeral was very special, and I was asked to create a track of Dad's music. So what I did was in a line, write a sentence with the songs so they would spell out a tribute. I made a ten minute CD of his music that spelled out his life.

But you know I walked down that aisle in my new black suit as I said not goodbye, but so long to my friend, my father, my dad, my hero who continued to believe what is right shall prevail. He also believed no matter what obstacles you have to go through, to keep climbing up that hill, and when you fall, like so many of us do, you get back up and you go harder because now you know you need a bit more to get up and over.

You know today is my birthday, and I realize that the greatest thing in this world is our life and time because the both of them together is important, just like Dad said "the one makes the other possible, it takes two to make life's troubles for the man and the woman."

I've already this week walked into stores and heard Dad's music playing. I recall one day I was shopping and I filled up my basket with food, and I was walking along when a song by Dad came on the radio in the store. I just could not contain myself. I tried to get it together, but I just couldn't and I ran out the store, jumped in my car and began to drive home. It was embarrassing to say the least, but it took some time for me to listen to his music without getting emotional. So what I did was everyday for about three months, I began turning on the CD player to hear his songs so much until I could take it.

After two years, I decided that I was going to write about him, and it took me another two years to get up the courage and start writing this work facing some truths that for some reason you try to avoid when you are here in this world. The very first thing I did was start listening to all of Dad's projects and he had a lot to say, but see I mentally placed myself inside of his thoughts to get a visual aspect.

So Jackie, Gena, Michelle and I went out and dined to discuss my plan to tell the world about Dad from our perspective and to get the record straight about him. I was here with him 43 years of my life. So I wanted to let everyone see from my eyes what I had experienced with my father and how he touched my life with his dreams that he shared with my siblings and I and why his songs meant the world to us for they told our story, his story.

All the love that Dad had for his family would grow as we started to spread his music and share it with our children. We settle down with our families and we convey that by showing love and faith in God, we are demonstrating to our children that their grandfather loved them all and carried himself with the greatest of class. He was not too proud, and he set the perfect example for us to see that dreams can come true. Also, he taught us that if we want to play music, doors have been opened and this is called a legacy.

As I went to the back room to grab one of Dad's tapes, something caught my eye - a tape that looked like it would not play. But I put it on and to my surprise, Dad's voice was singing new words! It's like I heard them before, but have I? I listened again very closely to the track only to realize that it is a new track that yes, I have not heard. It revealed that he was trying to figure out how to store his love forever so that he could spend all his life with his love.

Hearing this was overwhelming, and it gave me a great sense of power and love. I wanted him to be heard. I thought I would feel hurt, but no. Now I just feel so warm inside when I hear his voice, and it gives me inspiration to just smile and thank God for him and the time we shared with each other. I know my father will forever be in God's light shining through.

Dad has always been able to capture his audience because when his song would come on, you went with him for a moment in his life and his story, and you experienced some of what he had gone through. That is truly a great writer if you can see what he had explained and felt.

You know Dad wrote a song called *I Keep Coming Back to You*, and this shows that he had grown just as I have. You do this as the years pass you by. You learn from your mistakes, so you gather yourself and you strive to do better or your best.

As I'm going through my life trying to sort things out finding out what Dad's last wishes were and what he would want us to do, I said to myself, he always wanted the best, so I look to his words in his songs like *Give More Power to the People*. That was him living, being young, driving a cab, not making the right funds and the world that holds the power seems to not care. How can you be happy and smile and not have what it takes to take care of your responsibilities? Or what about *Give it Away*? It's a song about showing love for someone and not getting that same love back in return. At just a young age, he hadn't made the money yet, so he was just a struggling songwriter that was trying to make it. Or how about *Let Me Be the Man My Daddy Was*? He was trying as hard as he knew how to take care of his family only to come up short time after time.

This is how you despair and almost give up, but you don't. You wake up the next day and you continue to work harder. These are the things that make a man.

Just sometimes he is *A Lonely Man* who at the end of the trials and tribulations, ends up with someone that is perfect for him because God brought them. You see *Oh Girl* in your life that seems to have everything you need and is willing to take on the job of all jobs being a "mother of love" and take care of four children who at this time was a little damaged. During the most important years, they have been everywhere but in the right family settings - mother, father, and children setting.

What Do I Wish For - I think Dad would wish that we live a full life with God. He said, "there will never be any peace until God is seated at the conference table," and see it's not hard at all to know what Dad wants for us. I know this may be kind of weird to some people, but this is what he has left me, and knowing my father, he put his soul into everything he did.

When we used to eat at the Tropical Hut, Dad saw that and liked the décor, so he wanted the basement to look like that and he spent hours making it just right. He showed his godlike qualities in carpentry and building things up as we are taught, so he let him in to his heart as we should do.

This little boy wanted only to teach when he grew up so he could be like one of his educators that he adored. He grew from a young man who wanted to play his guitar his father and mother gave him on Christmas to becoming a man that wanted a record company of his own. During his teenage years, he fell in love with a young girl and saw that fathering children can be an enormous task at hand, but it's important to love your children the way a father should love them. He watched his dreams almost slip away, but continued fighting getting up off the floor with no teeth, and broken arms and legs. He continued to work hard, and the day came when he found someone that could mend his broken heart. He found that the true God makes a full circle and to be called by him is surely a life experience. I'm glad to have been a part of his life.

This book was written in the eyes of a child, and so it told of a knight and shining armor who came and saved me from this world that for some time wanted to devour my siblings as well as me, but my father never imagined anything but the best. He said he would get there, he just didn't know how and when, so he never gave up.

Dad's music will never die. It continues to multiply to the hundreds and even thousands, and even with no hard copies, just "clouds", his music will soar through space. No matter how far we go if not just a slither of sound will come racing toward your ear to enrich your day that is what music does to us all.

THE END

Michael has the first single of the continuing legacy tribute CD.

THE LEGACY

The Grandchildren

When I received the instruments from my father's studio, I couldn't do much with them. I just wanted to touch them because my dad did at one time. Actually, it made me even sadder for some time thinking that he could not play anymore. So I set them up in my studio.

I knew the first thing I needed to do was get the artists and the company together. It was very important that I continue the music in our family. Yes, this was what Mack started long ago.

The first thing I did was obtain some education in animation, so I took some classes because I needed to bring Dad back to life with animation and his music. Next, I knew we had talent in the family, so I just had to bring it out with whoever had it in them. I then started a website and set the studio up for recording.

The first artist I recorded was my wife, Jerraine Record. She has the talent of singing and playing the piano and violin. She is so talented. My father once said she sings like an angel. That's a compliment coming from him. After all, he had a voice that rocked them all.

One thing I had to do was make sure that I kept the Record family standard by keeping my music clean. As I mentioned earlier, some of today's music was getting dirty, and I vowed I wouldn't let that swallow me up. Jerraine came up with 10 beautiful songs. She didn't feel good at times, but I was proud she gave it her all. We released her CD in 2008. However, she found herself facing some serious medical issues. Thankfully, she made it through. Afterwards, I stuck by her side very closely.

I started working on my second CD with Charles "Charlie Boy" Jackson. At the time, he was a backup singer for a lot of mainstream artists like The Chi-Lites and others. Charlie Boy was from a group my father had produced in the 1970's called The Lost Generation. They had a hit song called *Mellow Mellow Right On*. Charlie Boy has such a wonderful voice. He is a first tenor like my father was. My wife and I wrote his CD and were almost done with it when he became ill. Even though Charlie Boy was an older fellow, we loved the way he could sing. The music that we wrote fit him so well. We are still waiting for him. His family said he is doing better, and we love him so much!

After Charlie Boy, the next artist I started working with was V. Ontario. He is Keisha Cole's uncle who sounds a lot like Luther Vandross. Luther died the same month my dad died and left a whole lot of fans, including me. I felt V. Ontario could make it with some of his beautiful music, but we could not see eye to eye on a lot of things. Nevertheless, this guy could really sing. He knew how to handle the stage microphone.

So I moved on to the next artist which was Derrick "Ricky Red" Maxwell, a Navy veteran from Chicago, Illinois and also an award winning vocalist of The National Veterans Creative Arts. He is a longtime friend and partner. We had put in time with the group, Elements of Time, back in the Stars Inn era. I knew that Ricky had stage training. He had sung with a lot of groups over the years, and he could really sing the blues. So we came up with a caption that his late brother, Ren'e, had said should be a song - *Get Your Roll On*. I loved the title of the song. I started writing, and Ricky came up with some lyrics as well. Greg Miller came up with the music, and we put the single out May 3, 2011. We are still working on the CD at this time.

We released a single by Laini Marisa called *Give It to Me* in 2013. I also plan to start working with the grandchildren of my dad to put the next generation of artists out.

Well, my nephew, Michael Record, came to live with me. Michael can rap very well, but remember, I will not produce any music that is immoral. It has to be clean and really come from the heart just like my dad would write. Michael does just that with his lyrics. He has a lot of character in his style.

My daughter, Cleo Record, who can rap better than any woman rapper I know, has a very good singing voice as well. Combining both rapping and singing makes her a very talented artist in a class of her own.

My sons, Jonathon, Joshua and Joseph Record, recently started learning songs on the piano. They seem to really have a "knack" for classical music. I would like to start recording them as pianists.

Now, I am also working with my two boys, Joshua and Joseph. Their group name is J-R-2. They are a young rap group coming out of Gary. They have great talent. Their CD will be released along with my dad's tribute CD which will have all of the family on it like my sister, Michelle. She was featured on a gospel CD that was released in 2009. She was a songbird. She will also be featured on Michael's CD as well.

My nephew, Shaqene Record, has developed quite a "natural ear" for the guitar, and my nephew, Myqui Record, has started writing his own songs and everything.

I have decided to work on my family's music at this time. I believe that my dad would have wanted me to give the family a chance to use the studio so we can keep the legacy alive.

Every time I hear my father's music, it just sends a chill through me. You see, Dad was such a gracious person and he loved his music. We as a family shared his music with him as well. When his album came out, we knew all the lyrics before the world would hear them. They were in our souls so to speak. We would fall asleep and wake back up with the same song playing. You see, Dad recorded at night mostly.

Steganography is the practice of concealing a file, message, or image of video within another file. I feel like that was going on with Dad; sometimes the message in his songs is right in front of me, but I can't seem to recognize it. It takes time to see the revelation and then it hits you just like you saw it all along. Dad's feelings were hidden in his songs because very rarely did he show that much emotion. Remember, he has always been laid back and quiet, but he found out how to hide his feelings right in front of the whole world. Imagine that, right in front of everyone and people just took it for a song and that's it.

I remember the last day I saw my sister alive. She was doing something for someone else as usual. She called me to pick up our nephew, Michael Record, that day. Michelle and Angela got to my house at eight or nine in the morning, and we went to Crown Point to pick up Michael. However, it was too early, so we decided to go and get some food. I told them let's go to Route 30 and grab some food, so we ended up eating chicken and we sat down and ate our last meal together (I myself never knowing it would be our last one) and it was pleasant.

After we picked Michael up and Michelle went out for a smoke, we left and went to my house. At that point, Michelle said she was not feeling good, so I told her to lie down if she wanted. So she laid down for about 30 minutes and then she said she wanted to go home, so she drove home. I talked to her later that night, and then she went to sleep.

I then got a call that informed me she was in the hospital that same night. That next morning when I got there, she was not conscious. I never

233

got to say anything else to my
sister, but when she was lying there
in the bed, I told her that I loved
her. I said I would do just what she
said - continue to write the book and
work on the music and video for the
tribute - because you see we want
everyone to know how much we loved
our father and maybe after we do
this, we will have another star born.

Michelle recorded her song for
the album, and we filmed her video as
well. Dad didn't live to see Michelle
pass, and I was happy for that. How
much can a father take? He had buried
two children already.

Michelle wrote songs that I will
move forward on until they are heard
because I love my whole family, and I
know this is what she would have
wanted. When my father was writing,
no one paid him any mind until he got
his chance to be heard. So any time
you write, take good care of your

234

music or songs. They could be the next hit, and how can any average person tell you otherwise?

I remember my sister (Michelle) walking down the aisle at her wedding as my father gave her away looking so beautiful in her white dress and my father so proud as any parent would be.

Michelle always just wanted to write something with her dad, so I made that possible. Before she left, we collaborated on a song and remake with Dad. It's called *Mr. Wonderful*. I was so happy to fulfill this before she went home, and she got to sing it with me. Yes, we videotaped it; she was so happy. Now Mom, Dad, Michelle, Darlene and Vincent are sleeping together now, and no man or woman can dictate what they can or cannot do. May they rest in peace.

My Father in Lites

Industry Awards & Special Honors

2 Diamond Records

10 Platinum Records

15 Golden Records

12 BMI Pop Awards

8 BMI R&B Awards

1 BMI Country Music Award

5 BMI Millionaires Club Awards

1 Grammy Award

Make A Wish Foundation

Armorbearer Award, Crusaders Church

Valuable Asset Award, Chicago Public Schools

Outstanding Service Award, Chicago Public Schools

2000 Pioneer Award, The Rhythm & Blues Foundation

ARTISTS WHO HAVE RECORDED

OR

SAMPLED EUGENE'S SONGS

Dad has had millions of people sing to his songs and thousands of people have recorded them or sampled them but here are some of the artists who have been successful.

2 Live Crew

Barbara Acklin

Beastie Boys

Bebe Winans

Beyoncé

Celo & Abdi

Common

Da La Soul

Dells

Dusty Springfield

239

Fantasia

Gene Chantler

George Benson

Ghostface Killah

Glenn Jones

Grover Washington Jr.

Helen Reddy

J. Holiday

Jackie Wilson

Jay-Z

Kanye West

Leo Sayers

M. C. Hammer

Paul Wall

Paul Young

Peaches and Herb

Phil Perry

Phoebe Snow

Public Enemy

Seal

Smokey Robinson

Joss Stone

The Dells

The Miracles

The Staple Singers

UB-40

Walter Jackson

Young Holt Unlimited

Young Trigger

Young-Holt Trio

And there are many, many more…..

Songs Eugene wrote or co-wrote

Dad has written over 300 songs and because of sampling and remakes, they have duplicated to over 1000's so here are some of his songs you can look up and listen to.

Are You My Woman

Baby Mama

Bad Motor Scooter

Bill Murray

Coldest Days of My Life

Come To My Party

Crazy in Love

For God Sake Give More Power To The People

From The Teacher To The Preacher

Have You Seen Her

Heavenly Body

Here Comes The Sun

Homely Girl

Hot On A Thing Called Love

I Like Your Lovin

ILL Bake Me A Man

I Touched A Dream

If Everybody Looked The Same

Just Pray

Just Two Teenage Kids

Lady Lady Lady

Laying Beside You

Let Me Be The Man My Daddy Was

Letter To Myself

Little Girl

Lonely Man

Love Makes A Woman

Magnetism

Marriage License

Mother of Love

Never Speak To A Stanger

Oh Girl

Oh Let Me Be The Man My Daddy Was

Soulful Strut

Stoned Out of My Mind

Toby

We Are Neighbors

We Need Order

Welcome To My Fantasy

What Do I Wish For

My Father in Lites

And Many, Many More........

EUGENE RECORD THE PRODUCER

Dad Produced or Co-Produced these Works

Of course Eugene produced every Chi-Lites successful album. When Dad produced an album, he used all of his talents. He would arrange, write, play instruments and sometimes sing on the tracks. This would ensure the song's success, and great sound. These are just some of his producing works.

Barbara Acklin-Love Make's A Woman

Barbara Acklin-Someone Else's Arms

Gene Chandler-The Two Sides of Gene Chandler

Ginji James-Love Is A Merry-Go-Round

Herman-I've Made Up My Mind

Jackie Wilson- Do Your Thing

Jackie Wilson- You Got Me Walking

Jackie Wilson-It's All A Part Love

Lowrell-Lowrell

-Mellow Mellow Right On

Robin Angel-Robin Angel

The Dells-I Touched A Dream

The Dells-Whatever Turns You On

The Lost Generation-The Sly, Slick & The Wicked

Young-Holt Unlimited-Soulful Strut

The Chi-Lites LP's Dad Produced

Give It Away

I Like Your Lovin' Do You Like Mine

For God's Sake Give More Power To The People

A Lonely Man

A Letter To Myself

Chi-Lites

Toby

Half A Love

Heavenly Body

Me & You

Bottom's Up

Steppin' Out

Eugene Record Discography

Dad finally released his solo albums with Warner Brothers and his own publishing company named after his daughters Angela and Michelle, AngelShell. These albums have been re-released and are selling all over the world to his true fans and great music lovers.

1976 The Eugene Record-Eugene Record

The Eugene Record was the first album from the former Mr. Chi-Lite. It spawned the number 24 R&B chart hit *Laying Beside You*. He opened with his signature love music that he was known for. Even though it never went gold, it has become a standard in the clubs and stays very close to his other works. It has now been re-released in 2015.

1978 Trying to Get to You-Eugene Record

This was Eugene's second LP with Warner Brothers. It was promoted a little better than the first, though both the first LP and the second LP have a smooth sound. Eugene performed this on Saturday Night Live NBC. The LP was recorded with over fifty talented musicians and was recorded in four different studios that were known at that time to have a very solid sound: P. S. Recording Studios, Streeterville Studios, Paragon Studios and of course The Burbank Studios. The songs are so smooth as Eugene shows off his silky evening voice. A glass of wine, dim the lights and you have just got yourself some love. Or going on a trip and need some nice smooth riding music, then grab this and go.

1979 Welcome to My Fantasy-Eugene Record

This was the last LP on the Warner Brothers label. The company went with new writers to find a new sound for Eugene. The first song on this LP, *Where Are You*, Andraé Crouch and Patrick Henderson, which is a change for Eugene's sound. He also picked up a new writing partner, Barbara Bailey, a newcomer. The LP is more on the dance side and Eugene is known more for his love songs and with his voice, this pair was gold.

Let Him In-Eugene Record

Dad's dream of owning his label finally came true, but little did he know it would be Gospel.

Let Him In was the last musical piece my father released before he passed. This is by far the hardest he has worked on any project. The most time he has spent on any work, and he recorded almost all the instruments as well. Evergreen Records

Memories

The Chanteurs (L-R) Clarence Johnson, Robert Lester, Eddie
Reed, Sollie McElroy and Eugene Record performed all around
the city of Chicago. Later, Robert Lester and Eugene Record
would make up half of the original vocal group The Chi-Lites.

John H. Johnson, Eugene Record, Edward A. William and Joseph E. Porter III

Irv Rothblatt, Eugene Record, Benita Brazier, Stan Harris/Jackie & Eugene

The Dynamic Sounds Orchestra was the backing band for The Chi-Lites during the 1970's and was responsible for bringing those hits to life on stage. With The Chi-Lites' vocals and the talented sound of the band, The Chi-Lites were unstoppable on stage with the smashing drums and horns, to the tightest rhythm section that reminisces of The Bar-Kays. This high energy band took no prisoners when the show lights turned on. (L-R): Clifford Conley, Louis Minter, Norwood Gray, Kevin Thompson, Charles Carter, Milton Thomas, Dennis Howell, bottom l-r, Otis Gould, Ron Scott.

Brian Anthony Record Sr. on the set of TV One's
Unsung for the taping of The Chi-Lites' episode.

The Original Chi-Lites

Eugene Record, Marshall Thompson, Creadel Jones & Robert Lester

Dad and his loving wife Jacqueline

Charlie Boy Jackson, Eugene Record, Lowrell Simon, Diana Simon and Fred Simon

Eugene with his brother-in-law, Ray Thompson, and his cousin, Isham McClenney

Eugene with Jo Carol & his nephews (L-R) Guy, Andy & Lee

Eugene at his 60th birthday party at the Hyatt Regency in downtown Chicago, IL on December 23rd. (L-R) with wife: Jackie, mother-in-law: Amanda Sutton, and sister-in-law: Peggy Sutton.

Eugene in his Brunswick Records Vice President office in Chicago, IL on South Michigan Ave (Record Row). The Chi-Lites hold two of the gold albums they received. L-R Marshall, Robert, Creadel, and Eugene. On the wall are some of Dad's gold records he wrote for the label. *Soulful Strut, Love Makes A Woman, Have You Seen Her* and others.

Eugene spent most of his later days in the home studio recording. After 40 years of performing, recording, producing, writing, and arranging, he decided to retire with his last works "Let Him In."

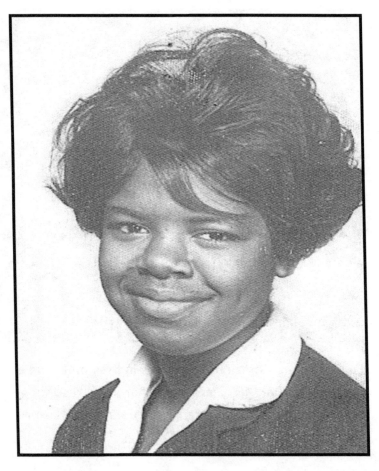

Eugene's youngest sister, Janet Record, was not born when the family portrait was taken.

Here is Eugene at his 60th birthday party with his family. (L-R) nephew: Melvin Thompson, brother-in-law: Ray Thompson, sister: Ruthie Thompson and his nephew: Byron Thompson.

(Back Row, L-R) Michelle Record, Lynda Camper, Robbin Camper and (Front Row) Brian Record at Amanda Sutton's house.

Gena Danice Record-Jones

(Back Row L-R) Brian Record, Eugene Record Jr., (Front Row L-R) Michelle Record and Angela Record in front of grandparents' house.

Eugene Jr. and his Grandfather Booker

Michelle Record-Protho
1963-2013

APPENDIX

Photo Courtesy of Jet Magazine page 256
Photo Courtesy of Brunswick Record page 259
www.soulmusic.com
Pruter, Robert. *Chicago Soul*. University of Illinois
Press, 1992.
Pruter, Robert. *Doowop*. University of Illinois Press, 1997.
www.discogs.com
www.nytimes.com/eugene-record
www.allmusic.com/artist/eugene-record
www.soultracks.com/eugene_record
www.amazon.com/eugene-record
www.imdb.com/name/nm1099611
www.encyclopedia.com
www.afrospear.com
www.jetarchives.com
Chicago Sun-Times
The New York Times
"The Chi-Lites Unsung TV Documentary." Accessed
March 15, 2015. http://www.youtube.com
www.brunswickrecord.com

Author: **Brian Anthony Record Sr.**

Growing up with my father gave me a lot of experience, and I owe Jehovah for still being here to actually write this book. I owe God, my six parents, my wife, children, family and friends for loving me!

Thank You!

My Father in Lites

CPSIA information can be obtained
at www.ICGtesting.com
Printed in the USA
LVHW08s1721080918
589551LV00008BA/65/P